**MidKent College**
LEARNING RESOURCE CENTRE

Medway Campus

Class No: _423   OXF_

## Return on or before the date last stamped below:

For renewals phone 01634 830633

# OXFORD
# PHOTO
# DICTIONARY

Oxford University Press

Oxford University Press
Great Clarendon Street, Oxford OX2 6DP

Oxford New York

Athens Auckland Bangkok Bogotá Buenos Aires
Calcutta Cape Town Chennai Dar es Salaam
Delhi Florence Hong Kong Istanbul Karachi
Kuala Lumpur Madrid Melbourne Mexico City
Mumbai Nairobi Paris São Paulo Shanghai
Singapore Taipei Tokyo Toronto Warsaw

and associated companies in
Berlin Ibadan

Oxford and Oxford English are trade marks of
Oxford University Press

ISBN 0 19 431360 3

© Oxford University Press 1991
Eleventh impression 2000

Editor: Jane Taylor

Printed in China

# Acknowledgements

**Location and studio photography by:** Graham Alder, Chris
Andrews, Martyn Chillmaid, Nigel Cull, Nick Fogden,
Paul Freestone, Gareth Jones, Mark Mason.

**The publishers would like to thank the following for
permission to reproduce photographs:** ABI Caravans Ltd;
Allsport (UK) Ltd/B Asset, S Bruty, R Cheyne, T Duffy,
S Dunn, J Gichigi, J Hayt, B Hazelton, H Heiderman,
J Loubat, A Murrell, J Nicholson, M Powell, P Rondeau,
H Stein; Animal Photography/S Thompson, R Willbie;
Ardea London Ltd/D Avon, I Beames, L Beames,
J Clegg, E Dragesco, M England, J Ferrero, K Fink,
D Greenslade, A Lindau, J Mason, E Mickleburgh,
P Morris, S Roberts, R & V Taylor, A Weaving, W Weisser;
Art Directors Photo Library/S Grant; Associated Sports
Photography; Clive Barda; Barnaby's Picture Library;
J Allan Cash Ltd; Bruce Coleman Ltd/J Anthony, E & B
Bauer, J Burton, M Dohrn, J Foot, N Fox-Davies,
M Kahl, G Langsbury, W Layer, G McCarthy, M Price,
A Purcell, H Reinhard, K Taylor, N Tomalin,
R Wilmshurst; Colorsport/Compoint; Cotswold Wildlife
Park; Cunard Line Ltd; Mary Evans Picture Library; Fiat
Fork Lift Trucks; Michael Fogden; Ford Motor Company
Ltd; Robert Harding Picture Library/Griffiths, G Renner;
Eric Hoskin/W Pitt; Hovertravel Ltd; Libby Howells; The
Hutchison Library/M Scorer; Rob Judges; Landscape
Only; Frank Lane Picture Agency/A Albinger, R Jones,
Silvestris, M Thomas, L West; Leyland Daf; London
Tourist Board; Mazda Cars (UK) Ltd; Metropolitan
Police; National Motor Museum, Beaulieu; Oxford
Scientific Films Stills/S Dalton, L Lauber, M Leach,
Partridge Films Ltd, Presstige Pictures, R Redfern,
F Skibbe, G Wren; Planet Earth Pictures/Seaphot/M Clay,
W Deas, D George, J George, K Lucas, J Lythgoe,
N Middleton, J Scott, J Watt; Renault UK Ltd; Rex
Features Ltd/N Jorgensen, J Tarrant; Rover Cars;
RSPB/G Downey, P Perfect, M Richards; Science Photo
Library/T Beddow, M Bond, Dr J Burgess, D Campione,
M Dohrn, T Fearon-Jones, V Fleming, NASA, S Patel,
R Royer, St Bartholomew's Hospital, J Sanford,
S Stammers, J Stevenson, S Terry; Shell UK Ltd;
Spectrum Colour Library; Swift Picture Library/T
Dressler, M Mockler; Toleman Automotive Ltd; Trust
House Forte; Wedgewood; World Pictures; Zefa/D
Cattani, Damm, D Davies, Goebel, C Krebs, R Maylander,
K Oster, J Pfaff, A Roberts, Rosenfeld, Selitsch.

**The publishers would like to thank the following for their
help and assistance:** Abingdon Hospital; Abingdon
Surgery; Russell Acott Ltd; Apollo Theatre; B & L
Mechanical Services, Eynsham; Douglas Bader Sports
Centre, St Edward's School; Barclays Bank; BBC Radio
Oxford; The Bear & Ragged Staff, Cumnor; H C Biggers,
Eynsham; Boswells of Oxford; Bournemouth
International Airport; British Rail; Cassington Builders
Ltd; Cheney School; Cherwell School; City Camera
Exchange, Brighton; Comet; Daisies, Oxford; Early
Learning Centre; Education & Sci Products Ltd; Elmer
Cotton Sports, Oxford; Eynsham Car Repairs; Faulkner &
Sons Ltd; For Eyes; Phylis Goodman Ltd, Eynsham;
Habitat Designs Ltd; W R Hammond & Son Ltd,
Eynsham; Hartford Motors Ltd; Headington Sports;
Heather's Delicatessen, Hove; Hove Delicatessen;
Inshape Body Studios Ltd; Johnsons of Oxford;
Littlewoods PLC; London Underground Ltd; Malin
Farms, Eynsham; P J Meagher, Eynsham; John Menzies
Ltd; North Kidlington Primary School; Ocean Village
Marina, Marina Developments PLC; Nigel Olesen BDS;
Options Hair Studio, Eynsham; Oxford Despatch; Oxford
Royal Mail & Post Office Counters; Paramount Sewing
Machines; Parkwood Veterinary Group; Payless DIY;
Phoenix One & Two; Qualifruit; Red Funnel Isle of Wight
Ferries; SS Mary & John School; Southampton Eastleigh
Airport; Stanhope Wilkinson Associates, Eynsham;
Summertown Travel; Texas Homecare, Oxford; Paul
Thomas; Richard Walton, Eynsham; Warlands, Cycle
Agents; Welsh National Opera; Western Newsagents,
Hove; Chris Yapp Consultants Ltd.

# Contents

| | |
|---|---|
| 1 Family Relationships | 45 A Science Laboratory |
| 3 The Human Body | 47 Shapes and Lines |
| 5 Physical Description | 48 Measurement |
| 6 What's the matter? | 49 The Classroom |
| 7 Health Care | 50 Space |
| 9 Describing Clothes | 51 The Weather |
| 10 Clothes | 52 The Temperature/The Seasons |
| 12 Dressing up | 53 The World |
| 13 Buildings | 55 The USA |
| 15 The Dining-room | 56 The British Isles |
| 16 The Living-room | 57 Prepositions |
| 17 The Bathroom | 59 The City |
| 18 The Bedroom | 61 Roads and Road Signs |
| 19 The Utility Room (*US also* Laundry Room) | 63 Vehicles |
| | 64 The Car |
| 20 The Kitchen | 65 Bikes |
| 21 Tools | 66 The Railway (*US* Railroad) |
| 22 The Garden | 67 At the Airport |
| 23 In the Market | 69 In Port |
| 25 At the Florist's | 71 Holidays (*US* Vacations) |
| 26 At the Newsagent's (*US* Newsstand) | 73 The Environment |
| 27 At the Delicatessen | 74 Hobbies |
| 28 At the Restaurant | 75 Musical Instruments |
| 29 At the Camera Shop (*US* Camera Store) | 76 Music and Theatre (*US* Theater) |
| 30 At the Hi-fi Shop (*US* Electronics Store) | 77 Sports |
| 31 Postal Services | 82 Keeping Fit (*US* Keeping in Shape) |
| 33 Numbers/The Date | 83 Verbs |
| 34 At the Bank | 87 Contrastive Adjectives |
| 35 American Money | 89 Animals |
| 36 British Money | 91 Fish and Reptiles |
| 37 Time | 92 Insects and other animals |
| 38 Emergency Services | 93 Birds |
| 39 Jobs | 94 Phonetic Symbols/Brit and US labels |
| 41 Daily Routine | 95 Index |
| 43 Office Verbs | 110 Exercises |
| 44 The Office | 125 Key to exercises |

# Family Relationships

**John's Family**

**1** grandmother

**2** grandfather

**3** aunt آنت عمه خاله

**4** uncle

**5** mother

**6** father

**7** father-in-law پدرشوهر

**8** mother-in-law مادرشوهر

**9** cousin کازن پسرعمه یاخاله یاعمو

**10** brother-in-law داماد یا شوهر خواهر

**11** sister لوف

**12** wife وایف همسر زن

**13** sister-in-law عروس یا زنی برادر

**14** niece میس بسربرادر بسر خوله لوف

**15** nephew فنو دختر خواهر، دختربرادر

**16** son سان فرزند پسر

**17** daughter دختر

**18** John is Ann's **husband**.

**19** Tom and Lisa are John and Ann's **children**.

**20** John and Ann are Tom and Lisa's **parents**.

**21** Mary and Bob Cox and Ian and Jane Hill are Tom and Lisa's **grandparents**.

**22** Tom is their **grandson**.

**23** Lisa is their **granddaughter**.

Helen Jones | Andrew Jones | Joan Cox | Alan Cox

Sally Jones | David Jones | Jill Jones | Mary Cox | Bob Cox | Ian Hill | Jane Hill

Rita Jones | Sam Jones | Paul Day | Tina Day | **John Cox** | Ann Cox | Carol King | Joe King

Lucy Day | Nick Day | Tom Cox | Lisa Cox | Mark King | Sue King

# The Human Body 1

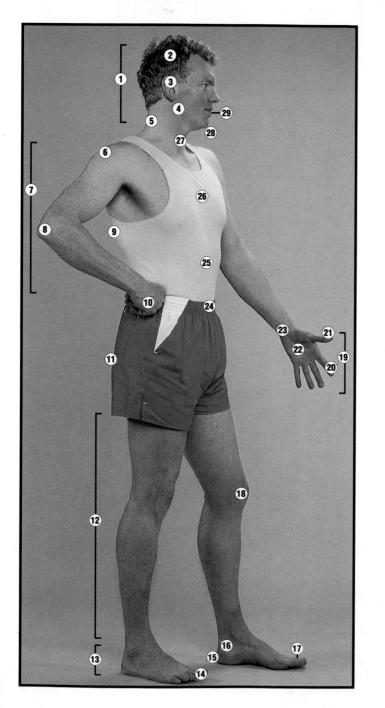

1 head
2 hair
3 ear
4 jaw
5 neck
6 shoulder
7 arm
8 elbow
9 back
10 fist
11 buttocks/bottom
12 leg
13 foot
14 toe
15 heel
16 ankle
17 nail
18 knee
19 hand
20 finger
21 thumb
22 palm
23 wrist
24 waist
25 stomach
26 chest
27 throat
28 chin
29 mouth

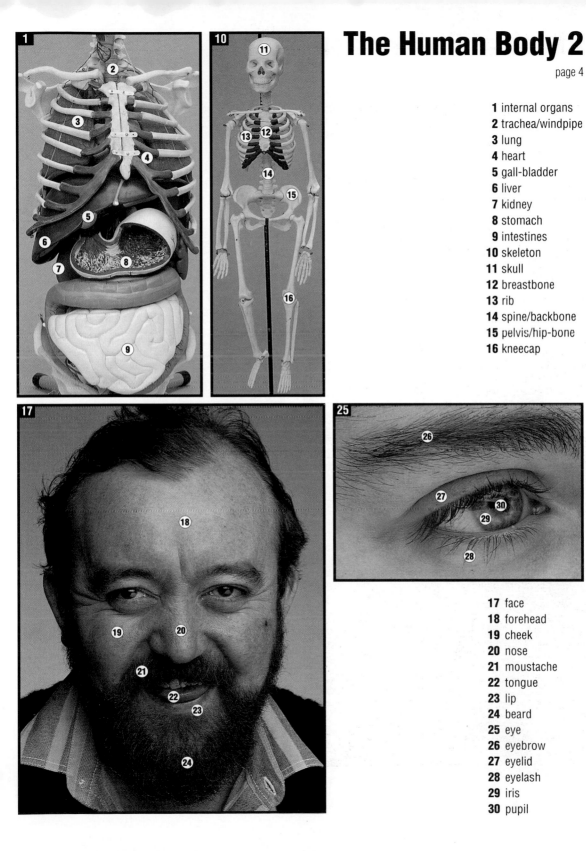

1 internal organs
2 trachea/windpipe
3 lung
4 heart
5 gall-bladder
6 liver
7 kidney
8 stomach
9 intestines
10 skeleton
11 skull
12 breastbone
13 rib
14 spine/backbone
15 pelvis/hip-bone
16 kneecap

17 face
18 forehead
19 cheek
20 nose
21 moustache
22 tongue
23 lip
24 beard
25 eye
26 eyebrow
27 eyelid
28 eyelash
29 iris
30 pupil

# Physical Description

**Age**
1 baby
2 child/(young) boy
3 teenager/teenage girl
4 adult/woman
5 adult/man
6 elderly (or old) man

**Hair**
7 bald head
8 short straight dark
9 short straight fair
10 short curly
11 short wavy
12 long red
   (Brit also ginger)
13 pony tail
14 fringe (US bangs)
15 long blonde
16 parting (US part)
17 plait (US braid)

18 tall
19 short
20 thin
21 fat

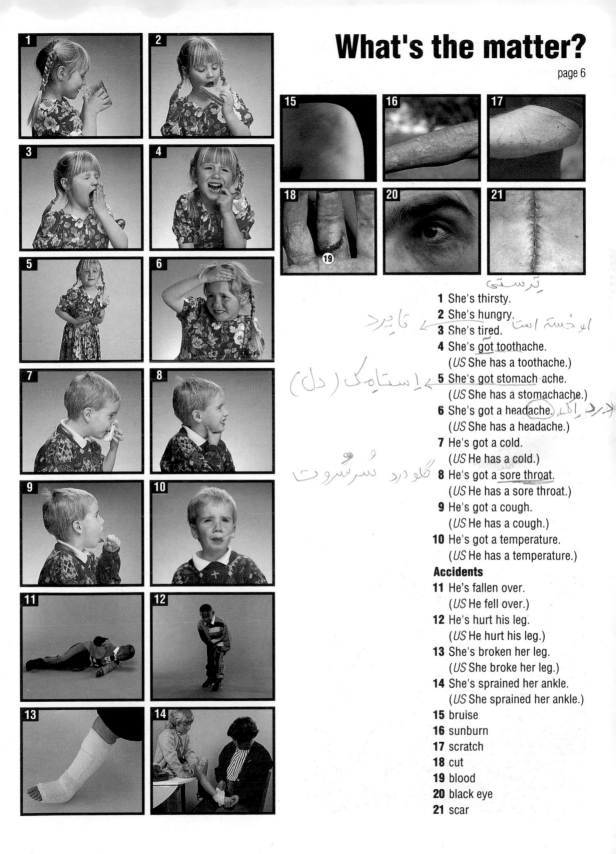

# What's the matter?

page 6

1 She's thirsty.
2 She's hungry.
3 She's tired.
4 She's got toothache.
 (*US* She has a toothache.)
5 She's got stomach ache.
 (*US* She has a stomachache.)
6 She's got a headache.
 (*US* She has a headache.)
7 He's got a cold.
 (*US* He has a cold.)
8 He's got a sore throat.
 (*US* He has a sore throat.)
9 He's got a cough.
 (*US* He has a cough.)
10 He's got a temperature.
 (*US* He has a temperature.)

**Accidents**

11 He's fallen over.
 (*US* He fell over.)
12 He's hurt his leg.
 (*US* He hurt his leg.)
13 She's broken her leg.
 (*US* She broke her leg.)
14 She's sprained her ankle.
 (*US* She sprained her ankle.)
15 bruise
16 sunburn
17 scratch
18 cut
19 blood
20 black eye
21 scar

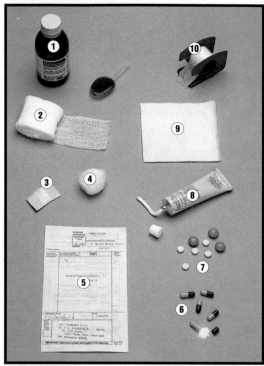

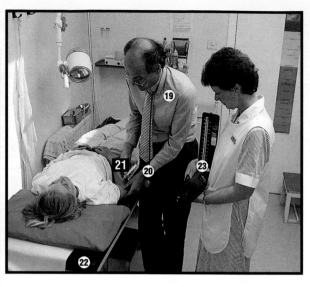

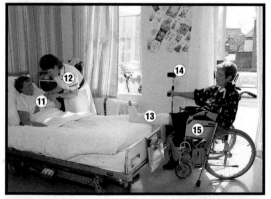

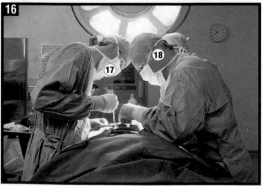

1 medicine
2 bandage
3 (sticking-)plaster
   (*US* Band-Aid)
4 cotton wool (*US* cotton ball)
5 prescription
6 capsule
7 pill/tablet
8 ointment
9 gauze pad
10 adhesive tape

**Hospital Ward**
**(*US also* Hospital Room)**
11 sling
12 nurse
13 plaster cast (*US* cast)
14 crutch
15 wheelchair

**Operation**
16 operating theatre
   (*US* operating room)
17 mask
18 surgeon

**Doctor's Surgery**
**(*US* Doctor's Office)**
19 doctor
20 stethoscope
21 injection
22 examination couch
   (*US* examining table/
   examination table)
23 blood pressure gauge

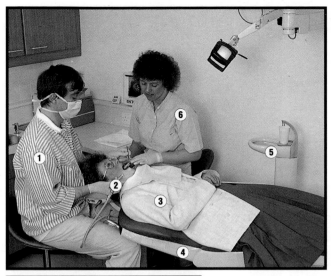

## At the Dentist's

1 dentist
2 drill
3 patient
4 dentist's chair
5 basin
6 dental nurse
   (*US* dental assistant)
7 gum
8 tooth
9 filling
10 X-ray (*also* x-ray)
11 front teeth
12 back teeth

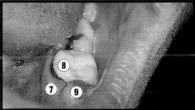

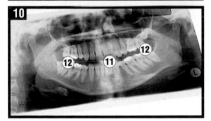

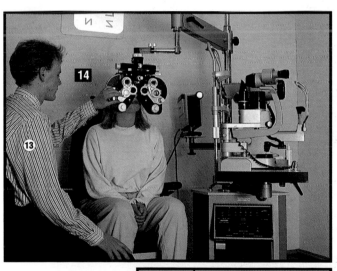

## At the Optician's

13 optician
14 eye test
15 (pair of) glasses
16 lens
17 bridge
18 frame
19 glasses case
   (*US also* eyeglass case)
20 contact lens
21 eye drops
22 contact lens cleaner

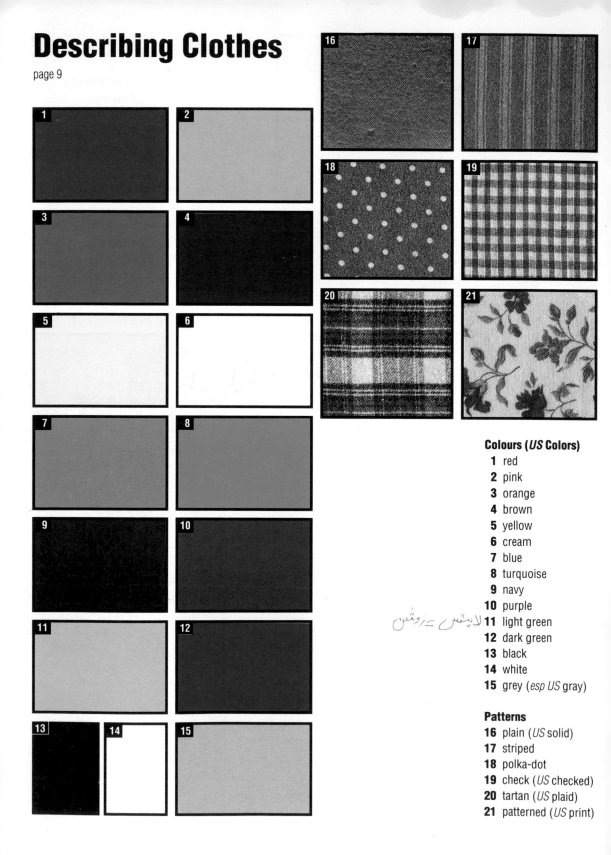

# Describing Clothes

**Colours (*US* Colors)**
1 red
2 pink
3 orange
4 brown
5 yellow
6 cream
7 blue
8 turquoise
9 navy
10 purple
11 light green
12 dark green
13 black
14 white
15 grey (*esp US* gray)

**Patterns**
16 plain (*US* solid)
17 striped
18 polka-dot
19 check (*US* checked)
20 tartan (*US* plaid)
21 patterned (*US* print)

| | |
|---|---|
| **1** school uniform | **13** boot |
| **2** cap | **14** scarf |
| **3** blazer | **15** glove |
| **4** trousers (*US* pants) | **16** umbrella |
| **5** T-shirt | **17** coat |
| **6** sweater | **18** suit |
| **7** jeans | **19** shirt |
| **8** jacket | **20** tie |
| **9** blouse | **21** handkerchief |
| **10** handbag (*US also* purse) | **22** raincoat |
| **11** skirt | **23** shoe |
| **12** briefcase | |

# Clothes 2 page 11

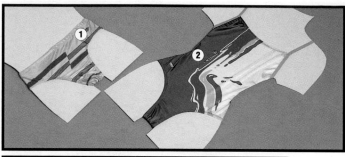

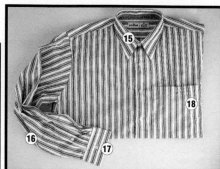

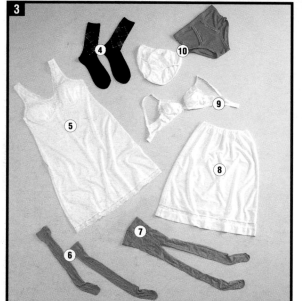

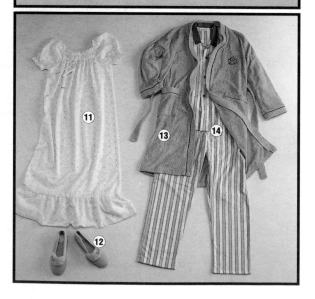

1 swimming-trunks
(*US* bathing suit)
2 swimsuit
(*US* bathing suit)
3 underwear
4 socks
5 full slip
6 stockings
7 tights (*US* pantyhose)
8 half slip
9 bra
10 pants (*US* underpants)
11 night-dress
(*US* nightgown)
12 slipper
13 dressing gown (*US* robe)
14 pyjamas (*US* pajamas)
15 collar
16 sleeve
17 cuff
18 pocket
19 buckle
20 heel
21 wallet
22 purse (*US* wallet)
23 shoelace

1 racing driver (*US* race car driver)
2 helmet
3 track suit (*US also* jogging suit)
4 trainer (*US* sneaker)
5 gypsy
6 scarf
7 cardigan
8 sandal
9 boxer
10 vest (*US* tank top)
11 belt
12 shorts
13 monster
14 sweatshirt
15 watch
16 witch
17 hat
18 sun-glasses
19 dress
20 make-up
21 lipstick

**Jewellery (*esp US* Jewelry)**
22 brooch (*US* pin)
23 bracelet
24 ring
25 chain
26 necklace
27 earring

# Buildings 1 page 13

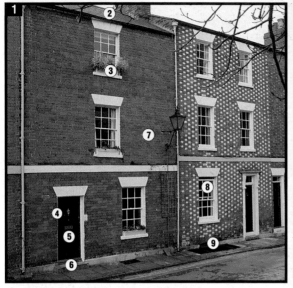

1 terraced house
  (*US* town house)
2 slate roof
3 window-box
4 knocker
5 letter-box (*US* mailbox)
6 doorstep
7 brick wall
8 sash window
9 basement window
10 block of flats
  (*US* apartment house)
11 top floor
12 balcony
13 first floor
  (*US* second floor)
14 ground floor
  (*US also* first floor)
15 car-park (*US* parking lot)

**Building Materials**
16 brick
17 stone
18 concrete
19 tile
20 slate
21 thatch
22 wood
23 glass

**1** detached house
(*US* one-family house)

**2** garage

**3** front door

**4** pillar

**5** shutter

**6** semi-detached house
(*US* two-family house)

**7** chimney

**8** window

**9** window-sill/window-ledge

**10** arch

**11** bay window

**12** concrete wall

**13** cottage

**14** thatched roof

**15** dormer

**16** porch

**17** wooden gate

**18** stone wall

**19** bungalow
(*US* ranch house)

**20** TV aerial (*US* antenna)

**21** drainpipe

**22** gutter

**23** tiled roof

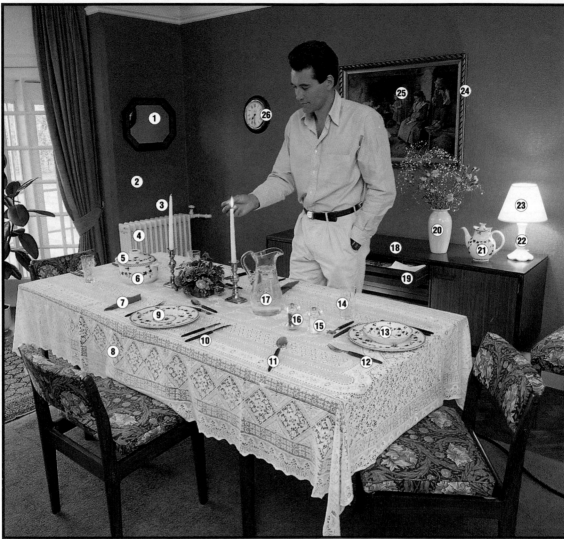

| | |
|---|---|
| **1** mirror | **14** glass |
| **2** wall | **15** salt |
| **3** candle | **16** pepper |
| **4** radiator | **17** jug (*US* pitcher) |
| **5** lid | **18** sideboard (*US* buffet) |
| **6** dish | **19** drawer |
| **7** napkin | **20** vase |
| **8** table-cloth | **21** coffee-pot |
| **9** plate | **22** lamp |
| **10** knife | **23** lampshade |
| **11** spoon | **24** frame |
| **12** fork | **25** painting |
| **13** bowl | **26** clock |

| | |
|---|---|
| **1** ceiling | **13** saucer |
| **2** mantelpiece (*US* mantel) | **14** cup |
| **3** fireplace | **15** teaspoon |
| **4** fire | **16** waste-paper basket |
| **5** log | **17** sofa (*esp US* couch) |
| **6** rug | **18** cushion |
| **7** carpet | **19** plant |
| **8** coffee-table | **20** curtains (*US* drapes) |
| **9** remote control | **21** wall unit |
| **10** biscuit tin (*US* cookie tin) | **22** armchair |
| **11** teapot | **23** television/TV |
| **12** tray | **24** video cassette recorder/VCR |

# The Bathroom

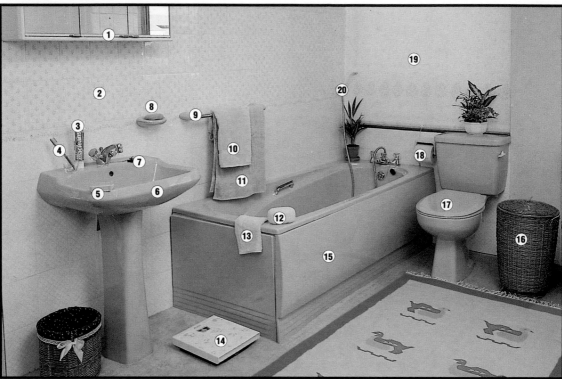

**1** bathroom cabinet
(*US* medicine chest/cabinet)
**2** tile
**3** tube of toothpaste
**4** toothbrush
**5** nail-brush
**6** wash-basin (*US* sink)
**7** plug (*US* stopper)
**8** bar of soap
**9** towel-rail (*US* towel rack)
**10** hand-towel
**11** bath-towel
**12** sponge
**13** flannel (*US* washcloth)
**14** (bathroom) scales (*US* scale)
**15** bath (*US* bathtub)
**16** laundry basket
(*US* hamper)
**17** toilet
**18** toilet paper
**19** blind (*US* shade)
**20** shower

**21** aftershave
(*US* after-shave lotion)
**22** electric razor
**23** razor
**24** razor-blade
**25** shaving-foam
(*US* shaving cream)
**26** shampoo
**27** comb
**28** talcum powder (*also* talc)

**1** dressing table (*US* dresser)
**2** bed-linen
**3** bed
**4** bedspread
**5** blanket
**6** sheet
**7** pillowcase
**8** hairbrush
**9** box of tissues
**10** bedside cabinet (*US* night table)
**11** mattress
**12** pillow
**13** headboard
**14** alarm clock
**15** poster
**16** light
**17** wardrobe (*US* closet)
**18** coat-hanger (*esp US* hanger)
**19** chest of drawers
　　(*US also* bureau)
**20** hair-drier (*or* hair-dryer)

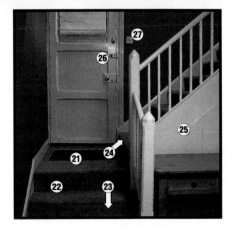

**21** doormat
**22** stair (*esp US* step)
**23** downstairs
**24** upstairs
**25** staircase
**26** lock
**27** light switch

| | |
|---|---|
| **1** detergent | **13** iron |
| **2** sink | **14** duster (*US* dust cloth) |
| **3** washing-machine | **15** light-bulb |
| **4** dustpan | **16** hook |
| **5** brush | **17** torch (*US* flashlight) |
| **6** bucket (*esp US* pail) | **18** scrubbing-brush |
| **7** vacuum cleaner | (*US* scrub brush) |
| (*Brit also* Hoover) | **19** cold(-water) tap |
| **8** mop | (*US* cold water faucet) |
| **9** ironing-board | **20** hot(-water) tap |
| **10** clothes-peg (*US* clothespin) | (*US* hot water faucet) |
| **11** flex (*esp US* cord) | **21** socket (*US also* outlet) |
| **12** plug | **22** clothes-line |

1 casserole
2 sieve (*esp US* strainer)
3 mixing bowl
4 cookery book (*US* cookbook)
5 washing-up liquid
   (*US* dishwashing liquid)
6 scourer (*US* scouring pad)
7 tea towel (*US* dish towel)
8 mixer
9 colander
10 tin-opener (*US* can opener)
11 ladle
12 rolling-pin
13 work surface (*US* counter)
14 fridge (*esp US* refrigerator)

15 freezer
16 mug
17 toaster
18 breadboard
   (*US* cutting board)
19 kettle
   (*US* electric teakettle)
20 cupboard (*esp US* cabinet)
21 oven glove (*US* pot holder)
22 oven
23 shelf
24 frying-pan
25 food processor
26 saucepan/pot
27 burner

آبین
فرانین
می تابه

# Tools

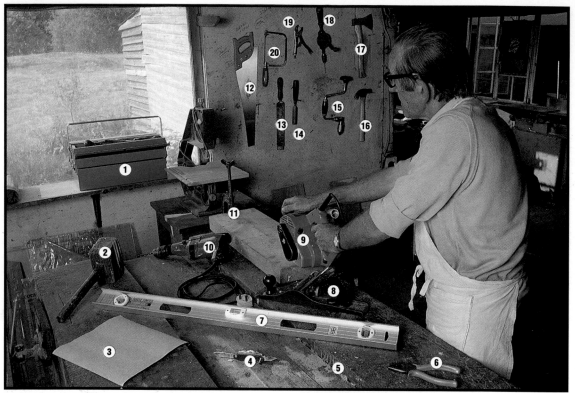

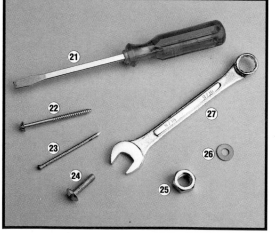

1 tool-box
2 mallet
3 sandpaper
4 penknife
  (*esp US* pocketknife)
5 workbench
6 pliers
7 spirit-level (*US* level)
8 plane
9 power saw
10 electric drill
11 vice (*US* vise)
12 handsaw (*esp US* saw)
13 file
14 chisel
15 brace
16 hammer
17 hatchet
18 hand drill
19 wrench
20 coping saw

21 screwdriver
22 screw
23 nail
24 bolt
25 nut
26 washer
27 spánner (*US* wrench)

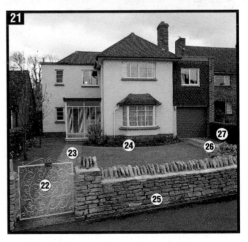

1 back garden (*US* backyard)
2 swing
3 grass/lawn
4 tree
5 lawnmower
6 watering-can
7 rake
8 shears
9 bush
10 flowerpot
11 patio
12 trowel
13 broom
14 bench
15 fence
16 barbecue
17 wheelbarrow
18 fork
19 spade
20 dustbin
   (*US* garbage can)

21 front garden
   (*US* front yard)
22 gate
23 path (*US* front walk)
24 flower-bed
25 wall
26 drive (*US* driveway)
27 hedge

# In the Market 1

page 23

## Vegetables

1 market stall (*US* stand)
2 garlic
3 green pepper
4 cauliflower
5 asparagus
6 radish
7 lettuce
8 beetroot (*US* beet)
9 potato
10 cucumber
11 onion

12 courgette (*US* zucchini)
13 watercress
14 carrot
15 Brussels sprout
   (*US* brussels sprout)
16 celery
17 broccoli
18 turnip
19 tomato
20 aubergine (*US* eggplant)
21 cabbage
22 paper bag

**Fruit**

1 melon
2 punnet of strawberries
  (*US* basket of strawberries)
3 bunch of bananas
4 apple
5 peanut
6 lemon
7 coconut
8 pineapple
9 orange
10 bunch of grapes

11 peach
12 bag of nuts
13 avocado
14 pawpaw (*esp US* papaya)
15 lychee (*also* litchi)
16 pear
17 lime
18 kiwi fruit
19 mango
20 plum
21 grapefruit
22 stack of baskets

**1** pine tree
  (*also* Christmas tree)
**2** trunk
**3** roots
**4** petal
**5** fern
**6** basket
**7** branch
**8** bark
**9** bunch of dried flowers
**10** dried flower arrangement
**11** leaf
**12** bonsai
**13** bulb
**14** daffodil

**15** chrysanthemum
**16** palm
**17** rose
**18** orchid
**19** stem
**20** freesia
**21** cactus
**22** pine cone
**23** daisy
**24** carnation
**25** tulip
**26** lily
**27** bud
**28** iris

## Confectionery (*US* Candy)

**9** box of chocolates
   (*US* box of chocolate)
**10** bag of sweets
   (*US* bag of candy)
**11** bar of chocolate
**12** twin-pack
**13** triple-pack
**14** packet of sweets
   (*US* pack of candy)
**15** packet of sweets
   (*US* roll of candy)
**16** packet of crisps
   (*US* bag of potato chips)
**17** chocolate
**18** sweets (*US* candy)
**19** crisps (*US* potato chips)

## Stationery

**1** reel of Sellotape
   (*US* roll of Scotch tape)
**2** ball of string
**3** packet of envelopes
   (*US* pack of envelopes)
**4** writing-paper
**5** set of coloured pens
   (*US* set of colored pens)
**6** roll of wrapping paper
**7** row of magazines
**8** pile of newspapers

# At the Delicatessen page 27

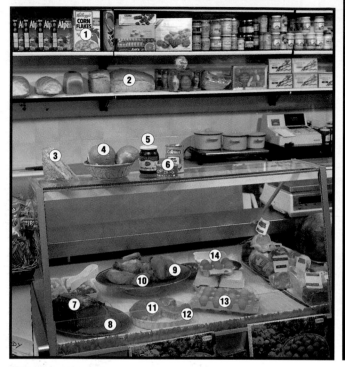

1 box of cereal
2 loaf of bread
3 sandwiches
4 roll
5 jar of jam/pot of jam
6 tin of tuna
  (*US* can of tuna)
7 joint of cooked meat
  (*US* roast)
8 slice of meat
9 roast chicken
10 chicken portion
  (*US* piece of chicken)
11 pie
12 piece of pie
13 dozen eggs
14 half a dozen eggs
15 biscuit (*US* cookie)
16 packet of biscuits
  (*US* package of cookies)
17 jam
18 tuna

19 pot of yoghurt
  (*US* container of yogurt)
20 tub of margarine
21 carton of orange juice
22 cheese
23 stuffed olives
24 pint of milk
25 bottle of mineral water
26 can of fizzy drink
  (*US* can of soda)
27 yoghurt (*esp US* yogurt)
28 margarine
29 butter

**Starters (*US* Appetizers)**
1 cherry
2 melon
3 smoked salmon
4 pâté with toast
5 tomato soup

**Desserts**
6 dessert trolley
 (*US* dessert cart)
7 fruit
8 apple pie
9 cheesecake
10 raspberry ice-cream
11 fruit cocktail
12 cream
13 chocolate gateau
 (*US* chocolate cake)

14 waiter
15 menu

**Main Courses**
16 roast beef
17 trout with almonds
18 steak
19 lamb chops

**Vegetables**
20 sweet corn (*US* corn)
21 mushrooms
22 salad
23 runner beans
 (*US* string beans)
24 peas
25 jacket potato
 (*esp US* baked potato)
26 boiled potatoes
27 chips (*US* French fries)

# At the Camera Shop (*US* Camera Store)

1 customer
2 receipt
3 cash register
4 tripod
5 telescope
6 shop assistant
  (*US* salesperson)
7 binoculars
8 slide projector
9 slide
10 negative
11 reel of film
  (*US* roll of film)
12 photo album
13 colour print
  (*US* color print)
14 black and white print

15 zoom lens
16 single lens reflex/SLR
  camera
17 lens
18 flash (gun)
19 35 mm* compact camera
20 built-in flash
21 camera case
22 strap
23 polaroid camera

*mm = millimetre*
  *(US millimeter)*

# At the Hi-fi Shop (*US* Electronics Store)

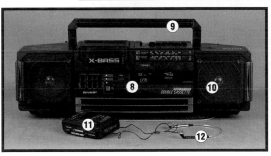

**1** camcorder
**2** microphone
**3** viewfinder
**4** (video)tape
**5** record
**6** cassette
**7** compact disc/CD
**8** radio cassette recorder
   (*US also* AM/FM
   cassette recorder)
**9** handle
**10** speaker
**11** Walkman
   (*Brit also* personal stereo)
**12** headphones

**13** stereo/stereo system
   (*US also* sound system)
   (*Brit also* hi-fi)
**14** turntable
**15** radio
**16** amplifier
**17** graphic equalizer
**18** cassette deck/tape deck
**19** compact disc player/
   CD player

# Postal Services 1 page 31

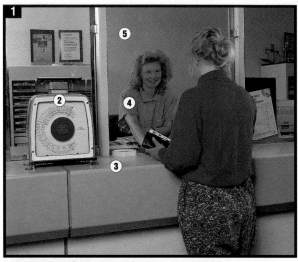

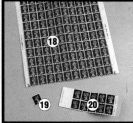

1 post office
2 scales (*US* scale)
3 counter
4 counter assistant
(*US* postal clerk)
5 window
6 collection
7 post office van
(*US* mail truck)
8 postman (*US* mailman)
9 mailbag
10 post (*US* mail)
11 letter-box/postbox
(*US* mailbox)
12 delivery
13 postbag
(*esp US* mailbag)
14 letter-box (*US* mailbox)
15 delivery by courier
(*US* delivery by messenger)
16 despatch-rider
(*US* messenger)
17 stamp machine
18 sheet of stamps
19 stamp
20 book of stamps

**British**          **American**

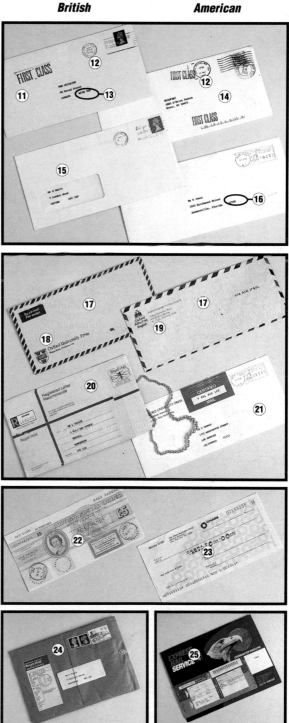

1 parcel (*esp US* package)
2 tape
3 label
4 greetings card
   (*US* greeting card)
5 letter
6 envelope
7 flap
8 postcard
9 message
10 address
11 first-class post (*Brit*)
12 postmark
13 postcode (*also*
   postal code) (*Brit*)
14 first class mail (*US*)
15 second-class post (*Brit*)
16 zip code (*US*)
17 airmail
18 address of sender (*Brit*)
19 return address (*US*)
20 registered post (*Brit*)
21 certified mail (*US*)
22 postal order (*Brit*)
23 money order (*US*)
24 Special Delivery (*Brit*)
25 Express Mail (*US*)

# Numbers/The Date

**1** one
**2** two
**3** three
**4** four
**5** five
**6** six
**7** seven
**8** eight
**9** nine
**10** ten
**11** eleven
**12** twelve
**13** thirteen
**14** fourteen
**15** fifteen
**16** sixteen
**17** seventeen
**18** eighteen
**19** nineteen
**20** twenty
**21** twenty-one
**30** thirty
**40** forty
**50** fifty
**60** sixty
**70** seventy
**80** eighty
**90** ninety
**100** one hundred
**101** one hundred and one
**1000** one thousand
**2210** two thousand, two hundred and ten
**1000000** one million

| JULY 1998 | | | | |
|---|---|---|---|---|
| Sunday | 5 | 12 | 19 | 26 |
| Monday | 6 | 13 | 20 | 27 |
| Tuesday | 7 | 14 | 21 | 28 |
| Wednesday 1 | 8 | 15 | 22 | 29 |
| Thursday 2 | 9 | 16 | 23 | 30 |
| Friday 3 | 10 | 17 | 24 | 31 |
| Saturday 4 | 11 | 18 | 25 | |

**1st** first
**2nd** second
**3rd** third
**4th** fourth
**5th** fifth
**6th** sixth
**7th** seventh
**8th** eighth
**9th** ninth
**10th** tenth
**11th** eleventh
**12th** twelfth
**13th** thirteenth
**20th** twentieth
**21st** twenty-first
**22nd** twenty-second
**23rd** twenty-third
**30th** thirtieth
**31st** thirty-first

MAY 3 1998

### British

3.5.98    3rd May 1998
3/5/98    3 May 1998

The third of May nineteen ninety-eight/
May the third, nineteen ninety-eight.

### American

5/3/98    May 3, 1998

May third, nineteen ninety-eight.

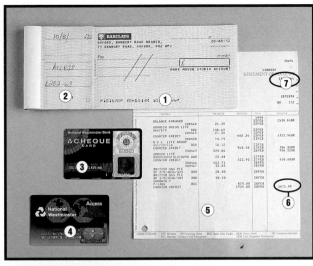

1 cheque book
   (*US* checkbook)
2 counterfoil/cheque stub
   (*US* check stub)
3 cheque (guarantee) card
   (*Brit only*)
4 credit card
5 bank statement
   (*esp US* monthly
   statement)
6 (bank) balance
7 (bank) account number
8 exchange rates
9 cashier (*US* teller)
10 changing a traveller's
   cheque (*US* cashing a
   traveler's check)
11 traveller's cheque
   (*US* traveler's check)
12 changing money
13 foreign currency
14 cashing a cheque
   (*US* cashing a check)
15 withdrawing cash
16 cash dispenser/cashpoint
   (*US* cash machine/
   automatic teller)
17 paying in
   (*US* making a deposit)
18 paying-in slip
   (*US* deposit slip)
19 withdrawal slip

# American Money

**1**

1¢/$0.01     5¢/$0.05     10¢/$0.10     25¢/$0.25

**1 coins**
**2** a penny
**3** a nickel
**4** a dime
**5** a quarter

**6 bills**
**7** a dollar bill
**8** a five dollar bill
**9** a ten dollar bill
**10** a twenty dollar bill
**11** a fifty dollar bill

**Paying (in) cash**
**12** twenty dollars
**13** seven dollars and
ninety-five cents/
seven ninety-five
**14** receipt
**15** total
**16** change

**6**

$1

$5

$10

$20

$50

HAPPY BIRTHDAY!

$7⁹⁵

**British Money**

| 1p/£0.01 | 2p/£0.02 | 5p/£0.05 | 10p/£0.10 | 20p/£0.20 | 50p/£0.50 | £1 | £2 |

£5

£10

£20

£50

**1 coins**
**2** a one pence piece/a penny
**3** a two pence piece
**4** a five pence piece
**5** a ten pence piece
**6** a twenty pence piece
**7** a fifty pence piece
**8** a pound coin
**9** a two pound coin

**10 notes**
**11** a five pound note
**12** a ten pound note
**13** a twenty pound note
**14** a fifty pound note

**How much is it?**
**15** twenty pence (*also* 20p)
**16** ten pence (*also* 10p)
**17** fifty pence (*also* 50p)
**18** three pounds
 eighty-two pence/
 three pounds eighty-two
**19** two pounds

# Time page 37

24 hours = 1 day
7 days = 1 week (wk)
365 days = 1 year (yr)
100 years = 1 century (c)

1 three o'clock
2 clock-face
3 minute-hand
4 hour-hand
5 second-hand
6 five past nine
(*US also* five after nine)/
nine o five
7 ten past nine
(*US also* ten after nine)/
nine ten
8 a quarter past nine
(*US also* a quarter after nine)/
nine fifteen
9 half past nine/nine thirty
10 twenty to ten/nine forty
11 a quarter to ten/
nine forty-five
12 ten to ten/nine fifty
13 twelve o'clock/midday
(*esp US* noon) *also* midnight
14 seven minutes past twelve
(*US also* seven minutes
after twelve)/twelve o seven
15 seven am (*US* A.M.)/
seven o'clock in the morning
16 five pm (*US* P.M.)/
five o'clock in the afternoon
17 eight pm (*US* P.M.)/
eight o'clock in the evening
18 eleven thirty pm (*US* P.M.)
half past eleven at night

# Emergency Services

### Police
**1** police station
**2** police car
**3** police officer

### Fire Brigade
(*US* **Fire Department**)
**4** fire-engine
**5** ladder
**6** water
**7** smoke
**8** fire
**9** fire extinguisher
**10** fireman
 (*esp US* fire fighter)
**11** hydrant
**12** hose

### Ambulance Service
**13** car accident
**14** ambulance
**15** injured man
**16** stretcher
**17** paramedic
**18** international code
**19** country code
**20** area code
**21** (tele)phone number
**22** (tele)phone box
 (*esp US* telephone booth)
**23** receiver
**24** phonecard (*Brit only*)
**25** slot
**26** dial

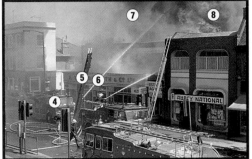

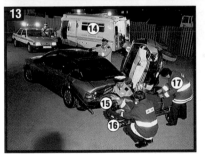

(18) (19)
00 44 1865 556767
01865 556767
(20) (21)

*In Britain the telephone number for the police, fire and ambulance services is 999. In the US the emergency number is 911.*

# Jobs 1

**1** artist
**2** gardener
**3** disc jockey (*US* disk jockey)
**4** newsreader (*esp US* newscaster)

**5** hairdresser
**6** pharmacist
**7** baker
**8** butcher

**9** farmer
**10** fisherman
**11** sailor
**12** soldier

**1** architect
**2** lorry driver (*US* truck driver)
**3** travel agent
**4** photographer

**5** computer programmer
**6** vet
**7** electrician
**8** carpenter

**9** welder
**10** plumber
**11** mechanic
**12** bricklayer

# Daily Routine page 41

1 He wakes up.
2 He gets up/He gets out of bed.
3 He goes downstairs.
4 He goes jogging.

5 He comes back.
6 He picks up the post (*US* mail).
7 He has a shower.
  (*esp US* He takes a shower.)
8 He gets dressed.

9 He has breakfast/He eats breakfast.
10 He leaves home.
11 He buys a newspaper.
12 He listens to music.

**13** He catches the train.
**14** He reads the newspaper.
**15** He starts work.
**16** He has a cup of coffee.
He drinks some coffee.

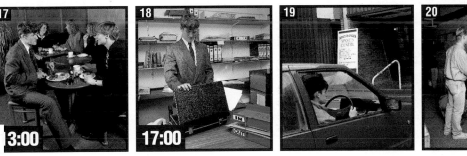

**17** He has lunch/He eats lunch
**18** He finishes work.
**19** He drives to the sports centre
(*US* health club).
**20** He meets his friends.

**21** He plays squash.
**22** He has dinner/He eats dinner.
**23** He watches television/TV.
**24** He goes to bed.

# Office Verbs

**1** She is dictating a letter.
**2** Dictaphone/dictating machine
**3** He is typing a letter.
   He is typing.
**4** He is stapling a cheque to a letter. (*US* check)

**5** She is filling in a form.
   (*US* She is filling out a form.)
**6** She is signing a letter.
**7** signature
**8** She is making a note of an appointment.

**9** He is filing.
**10** He is sending a fax.
   He is faxing a letter.
**11** It is printing.
   It is printing a copy.

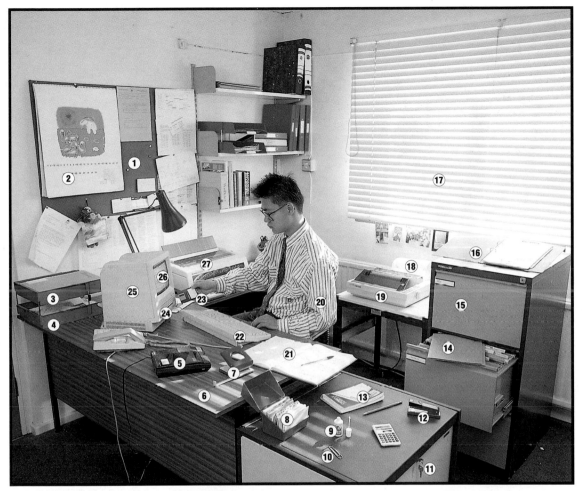

1 notice-board
(*US* bulletin board)
2 calendar
3 in-tray (*US* in box)
4 out-tray (*US* out box)
5 answering machine
(*Brit also* answerphone)
6 desk
7 hole-punch
8 card index (*US* card file)
9 Tipp-Ex
(*esp US* correction fluid)
10 paper-clip
11 key
12 stapler
13 notebook

14 file
15 filing cabinet
(*US* file cabinet)
16 ring binder
17 venetian blind
18 printout
19 printer
20 secretary
21 diary
(*US* appointment book)
22 keyboard
23 floppy disk
24 disk drive
25 personal computer/PC
26 screen
27 typewriter

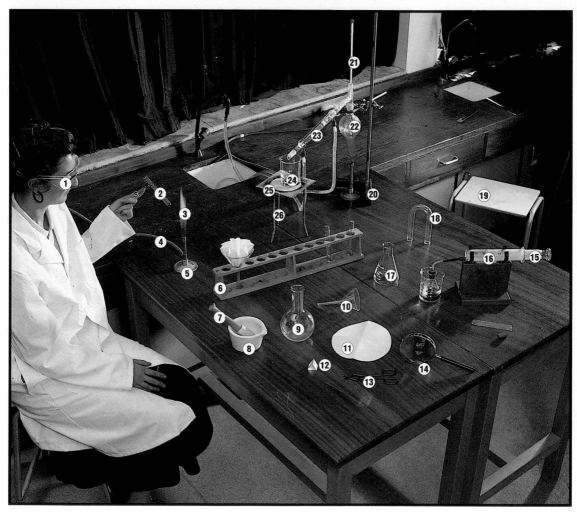

1 goggles
2 test-tube
3 flame
4 rubber tubing
5 Bunsen burner
6 rack
7 pestle
8 mortar
9 flat bottom flask
10 funnel
11 filter paper
12 prism
13 tongs
14 magnifying glass
15 plunger

16 syringe
17 conical flask
18 U-tube
19 stool
20 clamp stand
   (*US* ring stand)
21 thermometer
22 round bottom flask
23 condenser
24 measuring beaker
   (*US* graduated beaker)
25 gauze
   (*US* wire mesh screen)
26 tripod

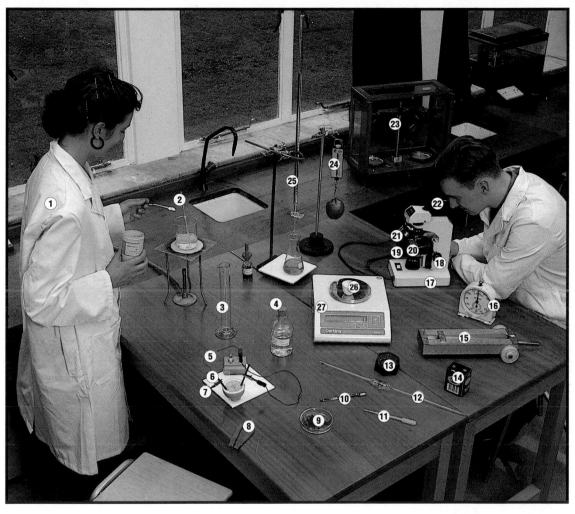

1 lab coat
2 glass rod
3 measuring cylinder
  (*US* graduated cylinder)
4 stopper
5 wire
6 electrode
7 crocodile clip
  (*US* alligator clip)
8 magnet
9 Petri dish (*US* petri dish)
10 spatula
11 dropper
12 pipette
13 weight

14 battery
15 trolley (*US* cart)
16 stop clock (*US* timer)
17 microscope
18 focusing control
  (*US also* focusing knob)
19 stage
20 slide
21 objective lens
22 eyepiece
23 balance/scales (*US* scale)
24 spring balance
25 burette
26 crucible
27 microbalance

# Shapes and Lines

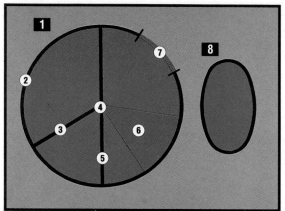

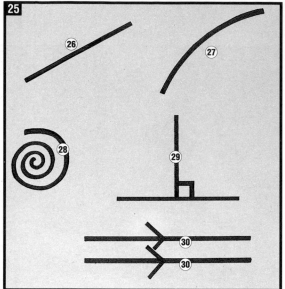

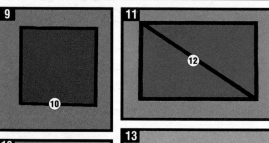

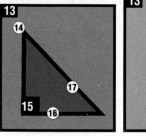

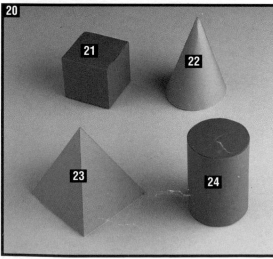

1 circle
2 circumference
3 radius
4 centre (*US* center)
5 diameter
6 sector
7 arc
8 oval
9 square
10 side
11 rectangle
12 diagonal
13 triangle
14 apex
15 right angle
16 base
17 hypotenuse
18 obtuse angle
19 acute angle
20 solid figures
21 cube
22 cone
23 pyramid
24 cylinder
25 lines
26 straight line
27 curve
28 spiral
29 perpendicular line
30 parallel lines

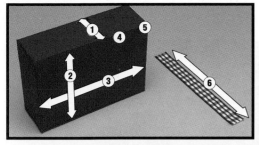

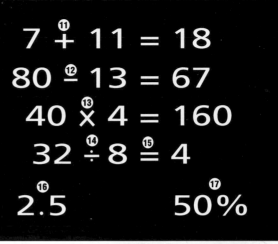

$$7 \overset{\text{⑪}}{+} 11 = 18$$
$$80 \overset{\text{⑫}}{-} 13 = 67$$
$$40 \overset{\text{⑬}}{\times} 4 = 160$$
$$32 \div 8 \overset{\text{⑮}}{=} 4$$
$$\overset{\text{⑯}}{2.5} \qquad \overset{\text{⑰}}{50\%}$$

1 depth
2 height
3 width
4 edge
5 corner
6 length
7 front
8 bottom
9 side
10 back
11 plus
12 minus
13 multiplied by/times
14 divided by
15 equals
16 two point five
17 fifty per cent
18 fractions
19 a quarter/ ¼
20 a third/ ⅓
21 a half/ ½
22 three quarters/ ¾
23 weight
24 10 grams*
25 kilogram*
26 capacity
27 millilitre (*US* milliliter)*
28 litre (*US* liter)*
29 millimetre (*US* millimeter)*
30 centimetre (*US* centimeter)*
   *\*These measurements are not
   usually used in US English.*

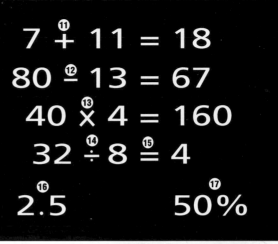

1000 grams (g) = 1 kilogram (kg)

1000 millilitres (ml) = 1 litre (l)

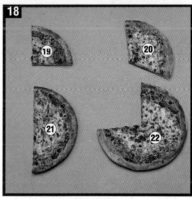

10 millimetres (mm) = 1 centimetre (cm)
100 centimetres = 1 metre (m)
1000 metres = 1 kilometre (km)

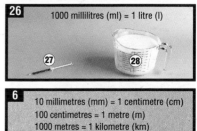

# The Classroom

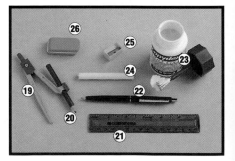

**1** blackboard (*US also* chalkboard)
**2** pupil (*esp US* student)
**3** textbook
**4** exercise book (*US* notebook)
**5** calculator
**6** set square (*US* triangle)
**7** protractor
**8** school bag
**9** (tiled) floor
**10** chair
**11** globe
**12** scissors
**13** easel
**14** paintbrush
**15** paintbox
**16** teacher
**17** picture
**18** map

**19** (pair of) compasses
    (*also* compass)
**20** pencil
**21** ruler
**22** pen
**23** glue
**24** (piece of) chalk
**25** pencil-sharpener
**26** rubber (*US* eraser)

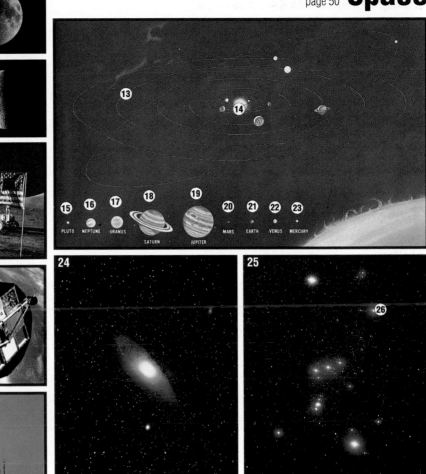

**1** new moon
 (*esp US* crescent moon)
**2** half moon
 (*US also* first quarter)
**3** full moon
**4** old moon
 (*US* half moon/last quarter)
**5** lunar module
**6** astronaut
**7** spacesuit
**8** lunar vehicle
**9** satellite
**10** rocket
**11** space shuttle
**12** launch pad

**The Solar System**
**13** orbit
**14** Sun
**The Planets**
**15** Pluto
**16** Neptune
**17** Uranus
**18** Saturn
**19** Jupiter
**20** Mars
**21** Earth
**22** Venus
**23** Mercury
**Outer Space**
**24** galaxy
**25** constellation
**26** star

# The Weather page 51

1 It's sunny.
2 It's raining. (*US also* It's rainy.)
3 It's snowing. (*US also* It's snowy.)
4 snow
5 It's windy.

6 It's misty.
7 It's foggy.
8 It's cloudy.
9 It's stormy.

10 thunderstorm
11 lightning
12 rainbow
13 It's bright.
14 It's dull. (*US* It's dark.)

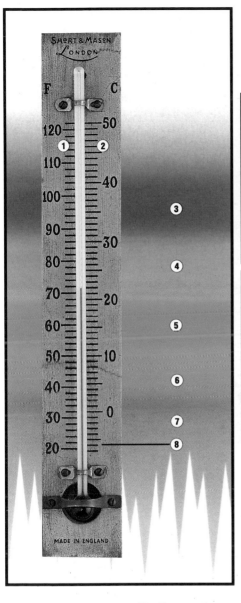

## The Seasons

9 in (the) spring

10 in (the) summer

11 in (the) autumn
   (*US* in the fall)

12 in (the) winter

## The Months

January

February

March

April

May

June

July

August

September

October

November

December

## The Temperature

1 degrees Fahrenheit

2 degrees Celsius
   (*or* centigrade)

3 It's hot.

4 It's warm.

5 It's cool.

6 It's cold.

7 It's freezing.

8 It's minus six (degrees).
   (*US* It's six (degrees)
   below zero.)

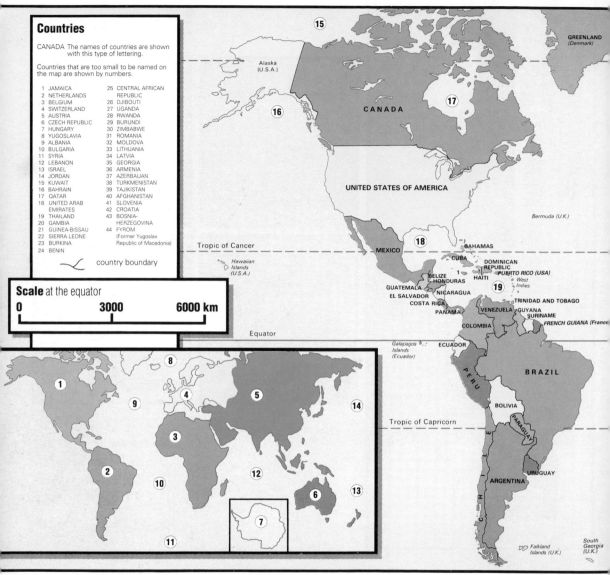

## Countries

CANADA The names of countries are shown with this type of lettering.

Countries that are too small to be named on the map are shown by numbers.

| | | | |
|---|---|---|---|
| 1 | JAMAICA | 25 | CENTRAL AFRICAN REPUBLIC |
| 2 | NETHERLANDS | 26 | DJIBOUTI |
| 3 | BELGIUM | 27 | UGANDA |
| 4 | SWITZERLAND | 28 | RWANDA |
| 5 | AUSTRIA | 29 | BURUNDI |
| 6 | CZECH REPUBLIC | 30 | ZIMBABWE |
| 7 | HUNGARY | 31 | ROMANIA |
| 8 | YUGOSLAVIA | 32 | MOLDOVA |
| 9 | ALBANIA | 33 | LITHUANIA |
| 10 | BULGARIA | 34 | LATVIA |
| 11 | SYRIA | 35 | GEORGIA |
| 12 | LEBANON | 36 | ARMENIA |
| 13 | ISRAEL | 37 | AZERBAIJAN |
| 14 | JORDAN | 38 | TURKMENISTAN |
| 15 | KUWAIT | 39 | TAJIKISTAN |
| 16 | BAHRAIN | 40 | AFGHANISTAN |
| 17 | QATAR | 41 | SLOVENIA |
| 18 | UNITED ARAB EMIRATES | 42 | CROATIA |
| 19 | THAILAND | 43 | BOSNIA-HERZEGOVINA |
| 20 | GAMBIA | 44 | FYROM (Former Yugoslav Republic of Macedonia) |
| 21 | GUINEA-BISSAU | | |
| 22 | SIERRA LEONE | | |
| 23 | BURKINA | | |
| 24 | BENIN | | |

country boundary

**Scale** at the equator

0      3000      6000 km

## Continents

**1** North America
**2** South America
**3** Africa
**4** Europe
**5** Asia
**6** Australia
**7** Antarctica

## Oceans

**8** Arctic
**9** North Atlantic
**10** South Atlantic
**11** Antarctic
**12** Indian
**13** South Pacific
**14** North Pacific

## Seas, Gulfs, and Bays

**15** Beaufort Sea
**16** Gulf of Alaska
**17** Hudson Bay
**18** Gulf of Mexico
**19** Caribbean Sea

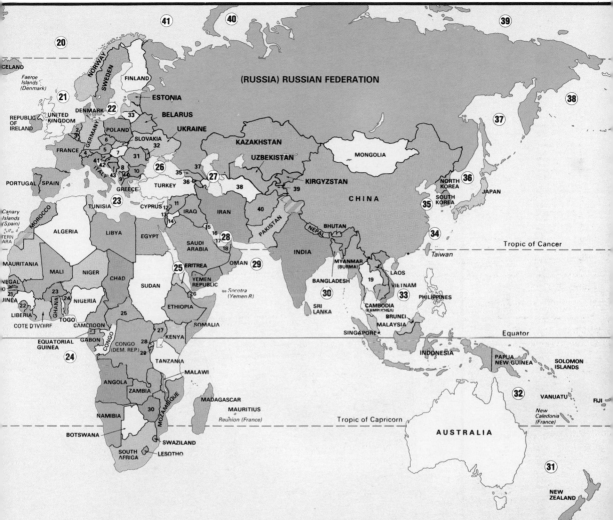

| | |
|---|---|
| **20** Norwegian Sea | **31** Tasman Sea |
| **21** North Sea | **32** Coral Sea |
| **22** Baltic Sea | **33** South China Sea |
| **23** Mediterranean Sea | **34** East China Sea |
| **24** Gulf of Guinea | **35** Yellow Sea |
| **25** Red Sea | **36** Sea of Japan |
| **26** Black Sea | **37** Sea of Okhotsk |
| **27** Caspian Sea | **38** Bering Sea |
| **28** Persian Gulf | **39** Laptev Sea |
| **29** Arabian Sea | **40** Kara Sea |
| **30** Bay of Bengal | **41** Barents Sea |

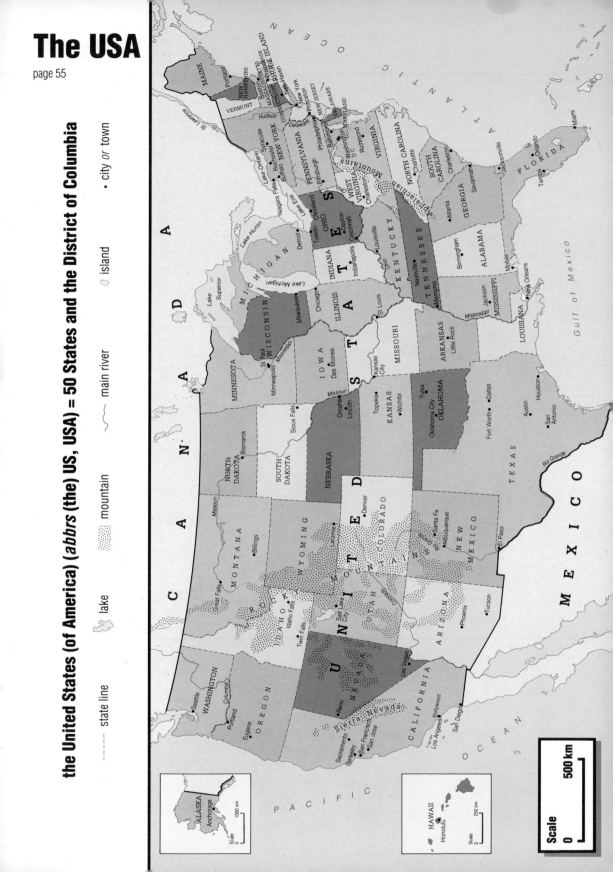

# The USA

## the United States (of America) (*abbrs* (the) US, USA) = 50 States and the District of Columbia

- - - - - state line

▨ mountain

◠ lake

∿ main river

◠ island

• city *or* town

international boundary
national boundary
■ capital city
• city or town

0    50    100 km

Shetland Islands

Orkney Islands

O u t e r   H e b r i d e s

SCOTLAND

Inverness

Aberdeen

A t l a n t i c
O c e a n

H e b r i d e s

Dundee
St Andrews
Stirling
Glasgow  Edinburgh
Berwick-upon-Tweed

NORTHERN
IRELAND

Londonderry

Belfast

Carlisle
Newcastle upon Tyne
Durham
Keswick
Middlesbrough

N o r t h
S e a

ISLE
OF MAN
Douglas

Irish Sea

York
Blackpool  Leeds
Bradford
Kingston upon Hull

Galway

Dublin

Anglesey
Holyhead
Caernarfon

Liverpool  Manchester
Sheffield
Chester
Stoke-
on-Trent  Derby  Nottingham
Shrewsbury
Birmingham  Leicester

Lincoln

ENGLAND

Limerick

WALES

Worcester
Hereford
Gloucester

Coventry
Warwick
Stratford-
upon-Avon

Norwich
Ely
Cambridge
Ipswich

Cork

REPUBLIC
OF IRELAND

Swansea
Cardiff

Bristol
Bath

Luton
Oxford  Colchester

London

Reading

Ramsgate
Canterbury
Dover

Strait of Dover

Taunton

Salisbury
Southampton

Brighton  Hastings

Eastbourne

Exeter
Bournemouth
Poole

Portsmouth
Isle of
Wight

Plymouth

Isles of
Scilly

E n g l i s h   C h a n n e l

| Great Britain (abbr GB) (also Britain) | = | England Scotland Wales |
|---|---|---|
| the United Kingdom (abbr (the) UK) | = | Great Britain Northern Ireland |
| the British Isles | = | Great Britain Ireland |

# Prepositions 1

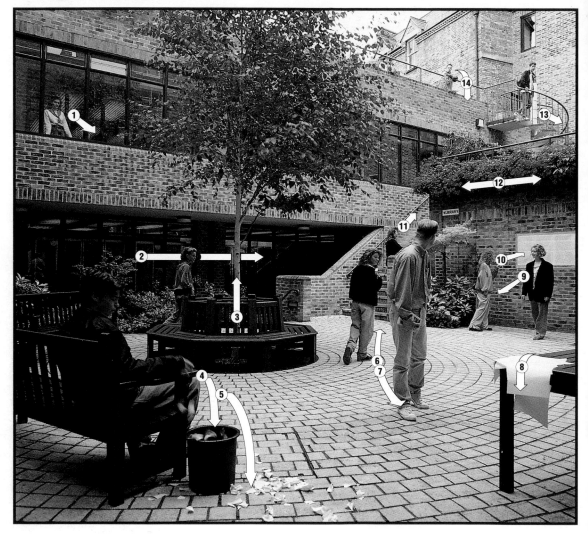

1 She is looking **out of** the window.
2 She is walking **across** the courtyard.
3 The tree is growing **through** the seat.
4 He is throwing some paper **into** the bin (*US* trash can).
5 He is throwing some paper **onto** the ground.
6 She is going **to** the library.
7 He is coming **from** the library.
8 The paper is falling **off** the table.
9 She is walking **away from** the notice (*US* sign).
10 She is walking **towards** (*esp US* **toward**) the notice (*US* sign).
11 She is walking **up** the steps.
12 The flowers are growing **along** the wall.
13 He is walking **down** the steps.
14 He is looking **over** the balcony.

1 The bush is **outside** the window.
2 The ribbon is **round** the basket (*esp US* **around** the basket).
3 The cassettes are **in/inside** the drawer.
4 The book is **against** the table.
5 The mug is **under/underneath** the table.
6 The table is **by/near** the fireplace.
7 The dried flowers are **in** the fireplace.
8 The clock is **between** the candles.
9 The candle is **on** the mantelpiece (*US* mantel).
10 The picture is **over** the mantelpiece (*US* mantel).
11 The plant is **on top of** the bookcase.
12 The ornament is **at the top of** the bookcase.
13 The plate is **in the middle of** the bookcase.
14 The books are **at the bottom of** the bookcase.
15 The plates are **above** the books.
16 The cups are **below** the teapot.
17 The teapot is **beside/next to** the plate.
18 The television is **in front of** the magazines.
19 The magazines are **behind** the television.

**1** road sign
**2** parking notice
 (*US* parking sign)
**3** letter-box/pillar-box
 (*US* mailbox)
**4** café (*also* cafe)
**5** police officer
**6** pavement (*US* sidewalk)
**7** manhole cover
**8** gutter
**9** kerb (*US* curb)
**10** street
**11** street corner
**12** shop (*esp US* store)
**13** traffic
**14** litter-bin
 (*US* trash can/garbage can)
**15** news-stand
**16** newspaper
**17** news-vendor (*Brit only*)
**18** department store
**19** flag

**20** advertisement
**21** bus shelter
**22** bus stop
**23** factory
**24** pedestrian crossing
 (*US* crosswalk)

**1** building
**2** park
**3** pram (*US* baby carriage)
**4** pushchair (*US* stroller)
**5** side street
**6** taxi/cab
**7** lamppost
**8** pedestrian
**9** railings
**10** street sign
**11** boat
**12** tower block
  (*esp US* skyscraper)
**13** sky
**14** skyline
**15** bridge
**16** pier
**17** river
**18** bank
**In the suburbs**
**19** traffic-lights
  (*US* traffic light)
**20** cyclist (*US* bicyclist)
**21** crossroads
  (*US* intersection)
**22** double yellow lines
  (*Brit only*)

**23** signpost
**24** car
**25** double-decker bus
**26** roundabout
  (*US* traffic circle/rotary)

# Roads and Road Signs 1 page 61

1 give way (*US* yield)
2 stop
3 no entry (*US* do not enter)
4 two-way traffic
5 no U-turn
6 speed limit
7 no left turn
8 bend to right
   (*US* curve to right)
9 cycle and pedestrian route
   (*US* bike and pedestrian path)
10 one-way street
11 service station
   (*US* service area)
12 turn right
13 roadworks (*US* road work)
14 dumper (truck)
   (*esp US* dump truck)
15 construction worker
16 pneumatic drill
   (*US also* jackhammer)
17 cone
18 JCB (*US* backhoe)
19 soil

1 motorway (*Brit*)
2 slip-road (*Brit*)
3 embankment (*Brit*)
4 hard shoulder (*Brit*)
5 inside lane/slow lane (*Brit*)
6 middle lane/centre lane (*Brit*)
7 outside lane/fast lane (*Brit*)
8 central reservation (*Brit*)
9 crash barrier (*Brit*)
10 flyover (*Brit*)

11 freeway/
   interstate highway (*US*)
12 exit ramp (*US*)
13 bank (*US*)
14 shoulder (*US*)
15 right lane/slow lane (*US*)
16 center lane/middle lane (*US*)
17 left lane/fast lane/
   passing lane (*US*)
18 median strip (*US*)
19 guardrail (*US*)
20 overpass (*US*)

21 underpass
22 footbridge
23 grass verge
   (*US* shoulder)
24 road (*US* highway)
25 junction
   (*esp US* intersection)

# Vehicles page 63

**1** transporter
**2** coach (*US* bus)
**3** tanker (*US* fuel truck)
**4** lorry (*US* truck)
**5** van
**6** cement-mixer
(*US* cement truck)
**7** pick-up truck
**8** fork-lift truck
**9** caravan (*US* trailer)
**10** jeep
**11** sports car
**12** saloon (*US* sedan)
**13** convertible
**14** estate (*US* station wagon)
**15** hatchback

1 filling-station
(*US also* gas station)
2 wing mirror
(*US* side mirror)
3 indicator (*US* turn signal)
4 headlight
5 number-plate
(*US* license plate)
6 exhaust-pipe
7 bumper
8 rear-light (*US* taillight)
9 boot (*US* trunk)
10 rear windscreen wiper
(*US* rear windshield wiper)
11 petrol pump (*US* gas pump)
12 hose
13 nozzle
14 bonnet (*US* hood)
15 engine
16 air filter
17 cylinder head
18 radiator grille

19 windscreen (*US* windshield)
20 dashboard
21 gear lever (*US* gearshift)
22 steering-wheel
23 fuel gauge
(*US also* gas gauge)
24 speedometer
25 ignition
26 clutch
27 footbrake
28 accelerator
(*US also* gas pedal)

# Bikes page 65

1 bicycle/bike
2 saddle (*esp US* seat)
3 pump
4 frame
5 crank
6 lock
7 spokes
8 chain
9 pedal
10 chain-wheel
11 valve
12 hub
13 gear lever
   (*US* gear changer)
14 reflector
15 cable
16 brake lever

17 tricycle
18 bell
19 handlebar
20 wheel

21 scooter
22 mudguard (*US* fender)
23 seat
24 top box (*US* top case)

25 motor cycle
   (*Brit also* motor bike)
26 accelerator/throttle
27 tyre (*US* tire)
28 engine
29 shock absorbers

**1** signal-box
(*US* signal tower)
**2** level crossing
(*US* grade crossing)
**3** engine
**4** coach (*US* passenger car)

**The Underground
(*US* The Subway)**
**5** exit sign
**6** platform
**7** line(s) (*esp US* track)
**8** train
**9** tunnel

**At the Station**
**10** ticket office
(*US* ticket counter)
**11** window
**12** queue (*US* line)
**13** bag
**14** suitcase
**15** timetable
**16** rucksack (*esp US* backpack)
**17** departures board
(*US* departure board)
**18** platform number
(*US* track number)
**19** ticket-collector
(*US* ticket taker)
**20** passenger
**21** entrance (to platform 10)
**22** barrier (*esp US* gate)

# At the Airport 1 page 67

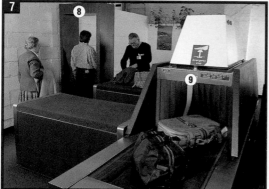

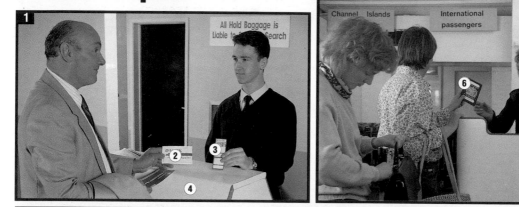

## In the terminal

1 check-in
2 airline ticket
3 boarding pass
4 check-in desk
   (*US* check-in counter)
5 passport control
6 passport
7 security
8 metal detector
9 X-ray scanner
10 duty-free shop
11 perfume

12 departures lounge
   (*US* departure lounge/
   waiting area)
13 seat
14 steward
   (*US* flight attendant)
15 gate
16 luggage reclaim
   (*US* baggage reclaim)
17 luggage
18 trolley (*US* cart)
19 customs
20 customs officer

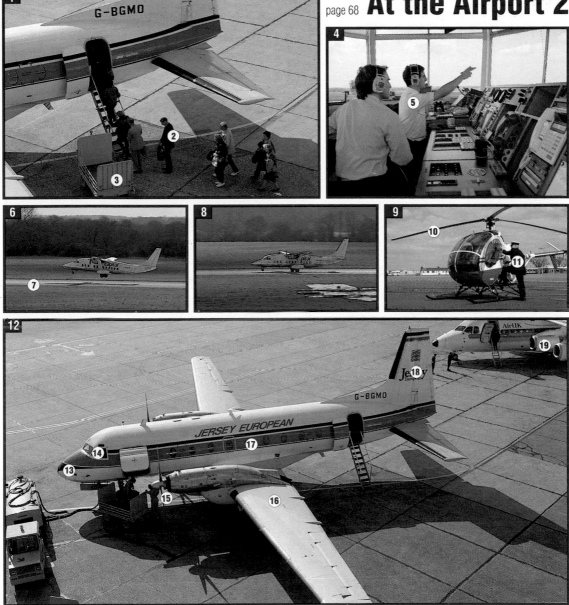

| | |
|---|---|
| **1** boarding | **10** rotor |
| **2** passenger | **11** pilot |
| **3** trailer | **12** plane |
| (*US* cart) | **13** nose |
| **4** control tower | **14** cockpit |
| **5** air traffic controller | **15** propeller |
| **6** take-off | **16** wing |
| **7** runway | **17** fuselage |
| **8** landing | **18** tail |
| **9** helicopter | **19** jet engine |

# In Port 1

1 sailing-ship
2 mast
3 sail
4 deck
5 cabin
6 cable (*US* line)
7 rowing-boat (*US* rowboat)
8 oar
9 barge

10 marina
11 motor boat
12 yacht (*US also* sailboat)
13 cabin cruiser
14 fishing boat
15 mooring
16 bow
17 stern
18 lifeboat
19 canoe (*US* kayak)
20 paddle

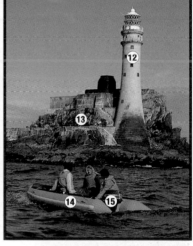

1 dock
2 crane
3 warehouse
4 cargo
5 ship
6 (oil-)tanker
7 hydrofoil
8 hovercraft
9 ferry
10 funnel (*US* smokestack)
11 liner (*esp US* ocean liner)
12 lighthouse
13 rocks
14 inflatable dinghy
    (*US* rubber raft)
15 outboard motor
16 anchor

# Holidays 1 (*US* Vacations) page 71

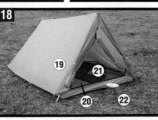

**1** hotel reception
  (*US* front desk)
**2** porter (*US also* bellhop)
**3** guest
**4** receptionist
**5** room key
**6** single room
**7** double room
**8** twin room
  (*US* room with twin beds)
**9** sightseeing
**10** tour guide
**11** party of tourists
**12** tourist
**13** castle
**14** country house
**15** village
**16** the countryside
**17** picnic
**18** camping
**19** tent
**20** groundsheet
**21** sleeping-bag
**22** camping stove
  (*US* camp stove)
**23** hiking
**24** hiker
**25** rucksack (*esp US* backpack)
**26** caravan site
  (*US* trailer camp)
**27** caravan (*US* trailer)

1 the seaside
   (*esp US* the beach)
2 holiday resort
3 beach
4 sea wall
5 promenade
   (*esp US* seafront)
6 cruise
7 sunbed
8 sunbather
9 sunshade
10 sailing
11 boating holiday
   (*US* boating vacation)
12 canal
13 fishing
14 angler
15 fishing-rod
16 pony-trekking
   (*US* horseback riding)
17 safari
18 parachuting
19 parachute
20 ballooning
21 hot-air balloon
22 hang-gliding
23 hang-glider
24 climbing
25 climber
26 harness

# The Environment page 73

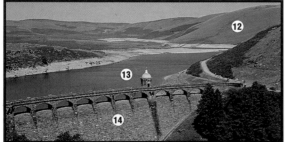

1 mountain
2 peak
3 valley
4 lake
5 forest
6 waterfall
7 stream
8 sea
9 rocks
10 beach
11 cliff
12 hill
13 reservoir
14 dam
15 desert
16 sand
17 sand-dune
18 plateau
19 wood (*esp US* woods)
20 farm
21 farmhouse
22 barn
23 pond
24 field
25 combine harvester
   (*US* combine)
26 cornfield
27 grain
28 tractor
29 plough (*esp US* plow)
30 furrow

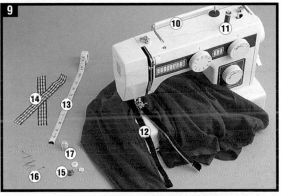

**1** painting
**2** drawing
**3** pottery
**4** stamp collecting
**5** stamp album
**6** making models
**7** kit
**8** model
**9** sewing
**10** sewing machine
**11** reel of cotton
   (*US* spool of thread)
**12** zip (*esp US* zipper)
**13** tape-measure
**14** ribbon
**15** button
**16** pin
**17** thimble
**18** embroidery
**19** needle
**20** thread
**21** knitting
**22** wool
**23** knitting-needle
**24** backgammon
**25** board
**26** draughts (*US* checkers)
**27** shaker
**28** dice
**29** chess
**30** pack of playing-cards
**31** jack/knave of clubs
**32** queen of hearts
**33** king of diamonds
**34** ace of spades

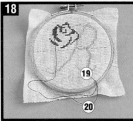

# Musical Instruments

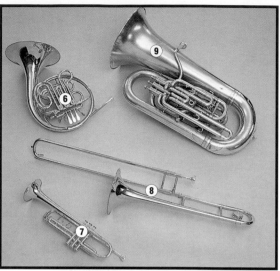

**Strings**

 **1** viola
 **2** bow
 **3** cello
 **4** violin
 **5** (double-)bass

**Brass**

 **6** French horn
 **7** trumpet
 **8** trombone
 **9** tuba

**Woodwind**

 **10** piccolo
 **11** recorder
 **12** flute
 **13** oboe
 **14** clarinet
 **15** bassoon
 **16** saxophone

**Percussion**

 **17** kettledrum
 **18** tambourine
 **19** drumsticks
 **20** bongos
 **21** cymbals
 **22** conga

**Other instruments**

 **23** accordion
 **24** keys
 **25** harmonica

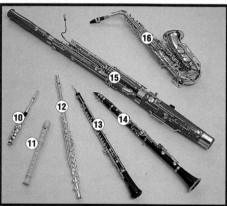

# **Music and Theatre (*US* Theater)**

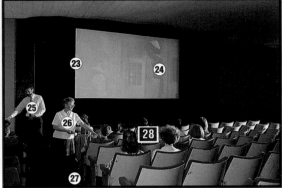

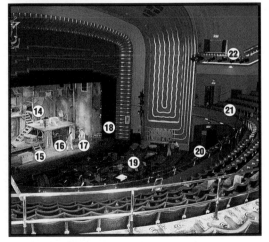

## Music
1 orchestra
2 musician
3 piano
4 conductor
5 baton
6 sheet music
7 pop group
8 (electric) guitar
9 singer/vocalist
10 drum
11 drummer
12 keyboard player
13 synthesizer

## The Theatre (*US* Theater)
14 scenery
15 stage
16 actor
17 actress
18 wings
19 orchestra pit
20 stalls (*US* orchestra seats)
21 circle/balcony
   (*US* mezzanine)
22 gallery (*US* balcony)

## The Cinema
## (*US* Movie Theater)
23 screen
24 film star (*US* movie star)
25 usher
26 usher (*Brit also* usherette)
27 aisle
28 audience

# Sports 1  page 77

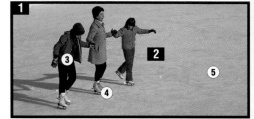

1 ice-skating
2 skate (*verb*)
3 skater
4 ice-skate
5 ice-rink (*esp US* rink)
6 skiing
7 ski (*verb*)
8 pole
9 ski
10 water-skiing
11 water-ski (*verb*)
12 water-skier
13 surfing
14 wave
15 surf (*verb*)
16 surfer
17 surfboard
18 windsurfing
19 windsurfer
20 sailboard
21 scuba-diving
22 (air)tank
23 snorkelling
    (*US* snorkeling)
24 snorkel
25 swimming
26 swim (*verb*)
27 swimmer
28 swimming-pool
29 dive (*verb*)
30 diver

1 baseball
2 batting helmet
3 batter
4 baseball glove/mitt
5 face mask/catcher's mask
6 catcher
7 crowd
8 basketball
9 net
10 shoot (*verb*)
11 American football
  (*US* football)
12 football
13 throw (*verb*)
14 rugby
15 tackle (*verb*)
16 hockey (*US* field hockey)
17 hockey player
18 hockey stick
19 hockey ball
20 volleyball
21 jump (*verb*)
22 squash
23 racket (*also* racquet)
24 badminton
25 shuttlecock
26 table tennis
  (*esp US* ping-pong)
27 table tennis bat
  (*US* paddle)
28 hit (*verb*)

1 darts
2 dartboard
3 aim (*verb*)
4 snooker
5 cue
6 table
7 pocket
8 bowling
9 bowling-alley
10 pins
11 golf
12 caddy
13 fairway
14 green
15 club
16 hole

17 boxing
18 corner
19 ring
20 ropes
21 boxing glove
22 punch (*verb*)
23 wrestling
24 wrestle (*verb*)
25 referee
26 judo
27 karate
28 chop (*verb*)

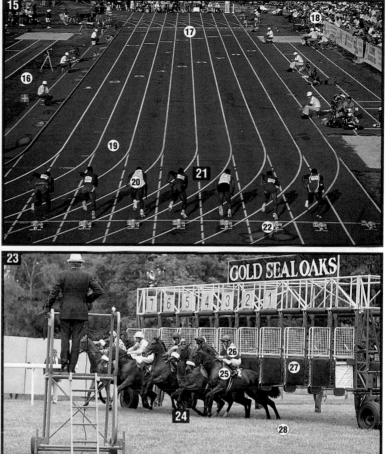

**1** gymnastics
**2** gymnast
**3** cycling
**4** cycle (*verb*)
**5** motor-racing
   (*US* auto racing)
**6** racetrack
**7** racing car (*US* race car)
**8** racing driver
   (*US* race car driver)
**9** riding
   (*US* horseback riding)
**10** ride (*verb*)
**11** rider
**12** saddle
**13** stirrups
**14** reins

**15** athletics
   (*US* track and field)
**16** field
**17** track
**18** spectators
**19** lane
**20** athlete
**21** run (*verb*)
**22** starting-block
**23** horse-racing
**24** race (*verb*)
**25** racehorse
**26** jockey
**27** starting-gate
**28** racecourse
   (*esp US* racetrack)

# Sports 5

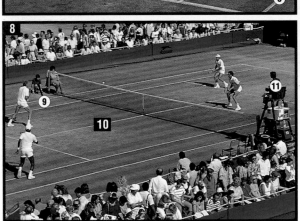

### Tennis

1 singles match
2 serve (*verb*)
3 server
4 baseline
5 service line
6 tramlines
   (*US* sidelines)
7 net
8 doubles match
9 ballboy
10 tennis-court
11 umpire

### Cricket

12 cricket match
13 wicket-keeper
14 batsman
15 pads
16 pitch
17 bowler
18 bowl (*verb*)
19 wicket/stumps
20 umpire
21 fielder
22 field

### Football
### (*esp US* Soccer)

23 scoring a goal
24 stand
25 linesman
26 score (*verb*)
27 goalpost
28 goal
29 miss (*verb*)
30 goalkeeper

**Keeping Fit (*US* Keeping in Shape)**

**9** throw (*verb*)
**10** catch (*verb*)
**11** swing (*verb*)
**12** rope
**13** climb (*verb*)
**14** wall bars
**15** gym/gymnasium
**16** vault (*verb*) ·
**17** mat
**18** vaulting-horse
**19** stretch (*verb*)
**20** bend over backwards (*verb*)
    (*US* bend over backward)
**21** kneel (*verb*)
**22** bend over (*verb*)
**23** blow a whistle (*verb*)
**24** whistle
**25** do a handstand (*verb*)
**26** skipping-rope
    (*US* jump rope)
**27** skip (*verb*)

**1** walk (*verb*)
**2** jog (*verb*)
**3** jogger
**4** trampolining
**5** fall (*verb*)
**6** trampoline
**7** instructor
**8** bounce (*verb*)

# Verbs 1 page 83

**1** He is **ironing**/He's **ironing** a shirt.
**2** He is **cooking**/He's **cooking** a meal.
**3** He is **cleaning**/He's **cleaning** a window.
**4** He is **sewing**. / He's sewing a

**5** He is **sweeping**/He's **sweeping** the path (*US also* walk).
**6** He is **tying up** a bag/He's **tying** a bag **up**.
**7** He is **digging**/He's **digging** the soil.
**8** He is **winding up** a hose/He's **winding** a hose **up**.

**9** She is **filling** a kettle (*US* an electric teakettle).
**10** The water is **boiling**.
**11** She is **pouring** the water into a teapot.
**12** She is **stirring** her tea.

 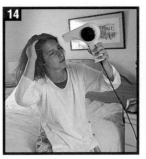  

**13** She is **washing** her hair.
**14** She is **drying** her hair.
**15** She is **combing** her hair.
**16** She is **brushing** her hair.

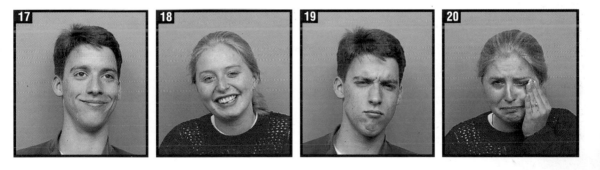

**17** He is **smiling**.
**18** She is **laughing**.
**19** He is **frowning**.
**20** She is **crying**.

**21** He is **sitting**.
**22** He is **standing**.
**23** He is **lying down**.
**24** He is **sleeping**.

# Verbs 3 page 85

1 They are **shaking** hands.
2 She is **kissing** the child.
3 She is **hugging** the child.
4 She is **waving** to the child.

5 She is **speaking** to him/She is **talking** to him.
6 They are **singing**.
7 They are **dancing**.
8 They are **clapping**.

9 She is **giving** him a present.
10 He is **taking** the present from her.
11 He is **opening** the present.
12 He is **reading** the book.

**13** She is **lifting** the suitcase.
**14** She is **carrying** the suitcase.
**15** She is **holding** the suitcase.
**16** She is **putting** the suitcase **down**.

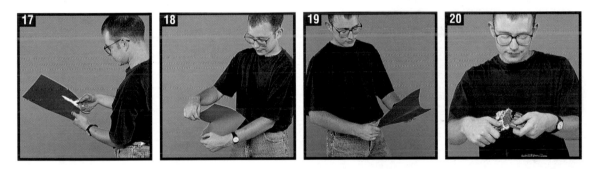

**17** He is **cutting** a piece of paper.
**18** He is **tearing** a piece of paper.
**19** He is **folding** a piece of paper.
**20** He is **breaking** a bar of chocolate.

**21** She is **pushing** a trolley (*US* cart).
**22** She is **pulling** a trolley (*US* cart).
**23** He is **lighting** a candle.
**24** The candle is **burning**.

# Contrastive Adjectives 1 page 87

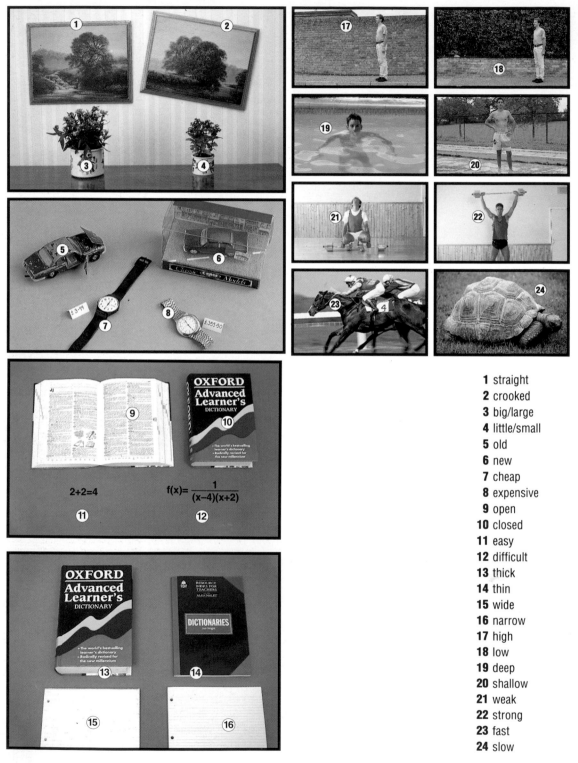

$2+2=4$

$f(x) = \dfrac{1}{(x-4)(x+2)}$

**1** straight
**2** crooked
**3** big/large
**4** little/small
**5** old
**6** new
**7** cheap
**8** expensive
**9** open
**10** closed
**11** easy
**12** difficult
**13** thick
**14** thin
**15** wide
**16** narrow
**17** high
**18** low
**19** deep
**20** shallow
**21** weak
**22** strong
**23** fast
**24** slow

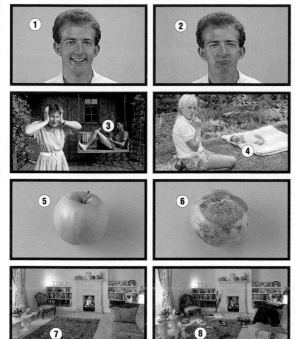

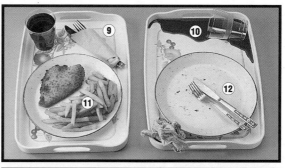

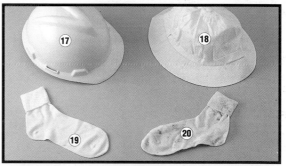

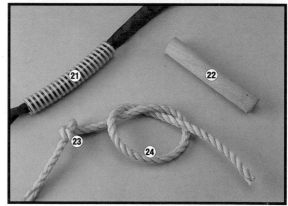

**1** happy
**2** sad/unhappy
**3** loud
**4** quiet
**5** good
**6** bad
**7** tidy (*esp US* neat)
**8** untidy (*esp US* messy)
**9** dry
**10** wet
**11** full
**12** empty
**13** light
**14** heavy
**15** rough
**16** smooth
**17** hard
**18** soft
**19** clean
**20** dirty
**21** hollow
**22** solid
**23** tight
**24** loose

# Animals 1 page 89

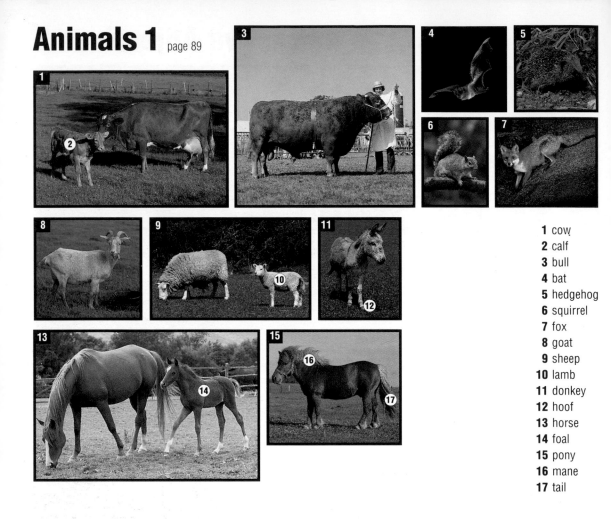

**1** cow
**2** calf
**3** bull
**4** bat
**5** hedgehog
**6** squirrel
**7** fox
**8** goat
**9** sheep
**10** lamb
**11** donkey
**12** hoof
**13** horse
**14** foal
**15** pony
**16** mane
**17** tail

# Pets

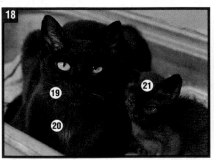

**18** cat
**19** whiskers
**20** fur
**21** kitten

**22** dog
**23** puppy
**24** paw
**25** hamster
**26** rabbit

1 deer
2 antler
3 wolf
4 bear
5 claw
6 polar bear
7 panda
8 kangaroo
9 pouch
10 camel
11 hump
12 llama
13 monkey
14 gorilla
15 zebra
16 lion
17 tiger
18 leopard
19 buffalo
20 horn
21 rhinoceros
22 hippopotamus
23 giraffe
24 elephant
25 tusk
26 trunk
27 seal
28 flipper
29 dolphin
30 whale

# Fish and Reptiles

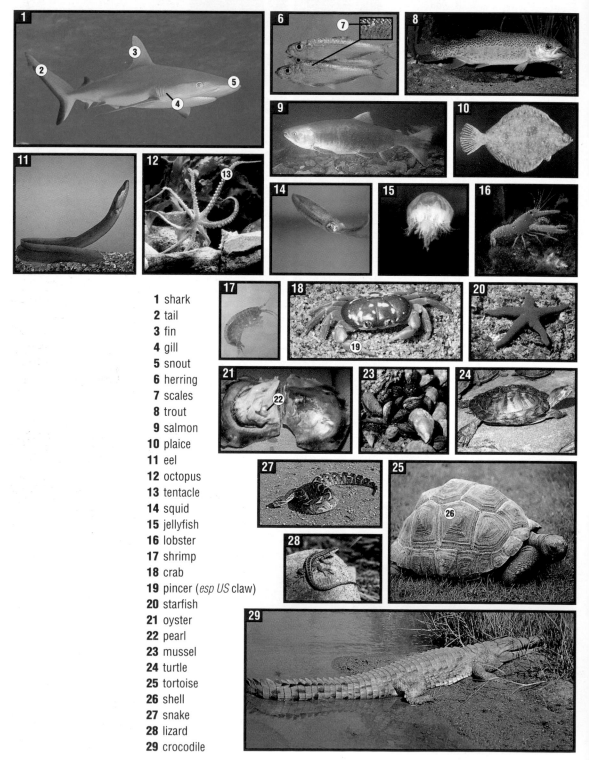

**1** shark
**2** tail
**3** fin
**4** gill
**5** snout
**6** herring
**7** scales
**8** trout
**9** salmon
**10** plaice
**11** eel
**12** octopus
**13** tentacle
**14** squid
**15** jellyfish
**16** lobster
**17** shrimp
**18** crab
**19** pincer (*esp US* claw)
**20** starfish
**21** oyster
**22** pearl
**23** mussel
**24** turtle
**25** tortoise
**26** shell
**27** snake
**28** lizard
**29** crocodile

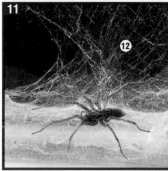

1 fly
2 bee
3 wasp
4 mosquito
5 dragonfly
6 butterfly
7 cocoon
8 caterpillar
9 moth
10 antenna
11 spider
12 (cob)web
13 beetle
14 ladybird (*US* ladybug)
15 ant
16 cockroach (*also* roach)
17 grasshopper
18 cricket
19 praying mantis
20 worm
21 slug
22 snail
23 scorpion
24 sting
25 frog

# Birds page 93

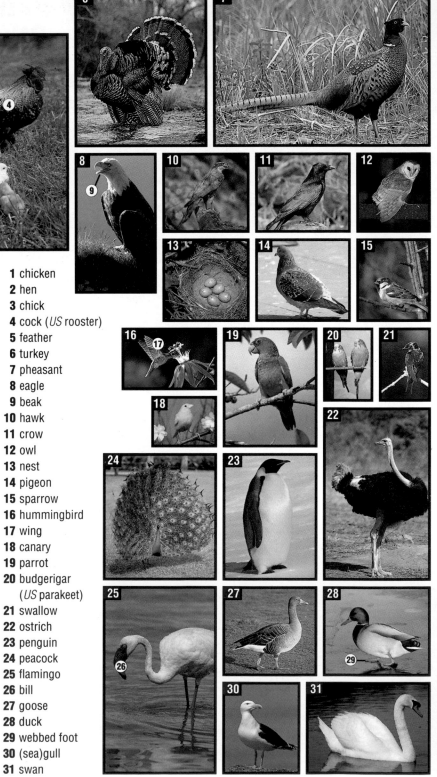

1 chicken
2 hen
3 chick
4 cock (*US* rooster)
5 feather
6 turkey
7 pheasant
8 eagle
9 beak
10 hawk
11 crow
12 owl
13 nest
14 pigeon
15 sparrow
16 hummingbird
17 wing
18 canary
19 parrot
20 budgerigar
   (*US* parakeet)
21 swallow
22 ostrich
23 penguin
24 peacock
25 flamingo
26 bill
27 goose
28 duck
29 webbed foot
30 (sea)gull
31 swan

## Vowels and diphthongs

| | | | | | | | | | | |
|---|---|---|---|---|---|---|---|---|---|---|
| 1 | iː | as in | **see** / siː / | | 11 | ɜː | as in | **fur** / fɜː(r) / |
| 2 | ɪ | as in | **sit** / sɪt / | | 12 | ə | as in | **ago** / ə'gəʊ / |
| 3 | e | as in | **ten** / ten / | | 13 | əʊ | as in | **page** / peɪdʒ / |
| 4 | æ | as in | **hat** / hæt / | | 14 | əʊ | as in | **home** / həʊm / |
| 5 | ɑː | as in | **arm** / ɑːm / | | 15 | aɪ | as in | **five** / faɪv / |
| 6 | ɒ | as in | **got** / gɒt / | | 16 | aʊ | as in | **now** / naʊ / |
| 7 | ɔː | as in | **saw** / sɔː / | | 17 | ɔɪ | as in | **join** / dʒɔɪn / |
| 8 | ʊ | as in | **put**/ pʊt / | | 18 | ɪə | as in | **near** / nɪə(r) / |
| 9 | uː | as in | **too** / tuː / | | 19 | eə | as in | **hair** / heə(r) / |
| 10 | ʌ | as in | **cup** / kʌp / | | 20 | ʊə | as in | **pure** / pjʊə(r) / |

## Consonants

| | | | | | | | | | |
|---|---|---|---|---|---|---|---|---|
| 1 | p | as in | **pen** / pen / | | 13 | s | as in | **so** / səʊ / |
| 2 | b | as in | **bad** / bæd / | | 14 | z | as in | **zoo** / zuː / |
| 3 | t | as in | **tea** / tiː / | | 15 | ʃ | as in | **she** / ʃiː / |
| 4 | d | as in | **did** / dɪd / | | 16 | ʒ | as in | **vision** / 'vɪʒn / |
| 5 | k | as in | **cat** / kæt / | | 17 | h | as in | **how** / haʊ / |
| 6 | g | as in | **got** / gɒt / | | 18 | m | as in | **man** / mæn / |
| 7 | tʃ | as in | **chin** / tʃɪn / | | 19 | n | as in | **no** / nəʊ / |
| 8 | dʒ | as in | **June** / dʒuːn / | | 20 | ŋ | as in | **sing**/ sɪŋ / |
| 9 | f | as in | **fall** / fɔːl / | | 21 | l | as in | **leg** / leg / |
| 10 | v | as in | **voice** / vɔɪs / | | 22 | r | as in | **red** / red / |
| 11 | θ | as in | **thin** / θɪn / | | 23 | j | as in | **yes** / jes / |
| 12 | ð | as in | **then** / ðen / | | 24 | w | as in | **wet** / wet / |

/'/ represents *primary stress* as in **about** / ə'baʊt /
/ˌ/ represents *secondary stress* as in **academic** / ˌækə'demɪk /

(r) An 'r' in parentheses is heard in British pronunciation when it is
immediately followed by a vowel-sound.
Otherwise it is omitted. In American pronunciation no 'r' of the
phonetic spelling or of the ordinary spelling is omitted.

## British and American labels

*Brit* motorway (*Brit*)
    used to show that an item is used only in British English

*US* zip code (*US*)
    used to show that an item is used only in American English

jug (*US* pitcher)
    used to show that an item (jug) which is used only in British
    English means the same as an item (pitcher) which is used only
    in American English

*Brit also* red (*Brit also* ginger)
    used to show that an item (red) which is used in both British
    and American English means the same as an item (ginger) which is
    used only in British English

*US also* blackboard (*US also* chalkboard)
    used to show that an item (blackboard) which is used in both
    British and American English means the same as an item
    (chalkboard) which is used only in American English

*esp US* sofa (*esp US* couch)
    used to show that an item which is used mainly in British
    English but can also be used in American English (sofa) means
    the same as an item (couch) which is the more usual term in American English

Aberconwy and Colwyn /ˌæbəˈkɒnwi ənd ˈkɒlwɪn/ **56**
Aberdeen /ˌæbəˈdiːn/ **56**
Aberdeenshire /ˌæbəˈdiːnʃə(r)/ **56**
above /əˈbʌv/ **58**/15
accelerator /əkˈseləreɪtə(r)/ **64**/28, **65**/26
accident /ˈæksɪdənt/ **6**, **38**/13
accordion /əˈkɔːdiən/ **75**/23
ace /eɪs/ **74**/34
across /əˈkrɒs/ **57**/2
actor /ˈæktə(r)/ **76**/16
actress /ˈæktrɪs/ **76**/17
acute angle /əˌkjuːt ˈæŋgl/ **47**/19
address /əˈdres; US ˈædres/ **32**/10, 18, 19
adhesive tape /ədhiːsɪv ˈteɪp/ **7**/10
adjective /ˈædʒɪktɪv/ **87**/**88**
adult /ˈædʌlt, also əˈdʌlt/ **5**/4, 5
administrative area /ədˌmɪnɪstrətɪv ˈeəriɪ/ **56**
advertisement /ədˈvɜːtɪsmənt; US ˌædvərˈtaɪzmənt/ **59**/20
Afghanistan /æfˈgænɪstɑːn; US æfˈgænɪstæn/ **54**
Africa /ˈæfrɪkə/ **53**/3
after /ˈɑːftə(r); US ˈæftər/ **37**/6, 7, 8, 14
after-shave lotion /ˈɑːftərʃeɪv ˌləʊʃn/ **17**/21
afternoon /ˌɑːftəˈnuːn; US æf-/ **37**/16
aftershave /ˈɑːftəʃeɪv/ **17**/21
against /əˈgenst, əˈgeɪnst/ **58**/4
age /eɪdʒ/ **5**
aim (verb) /eɪm/ **79**/3
air filter /ˈeə fɪltə(r)/ **64**/16
air traffic controller /ˌeə træfɪk kənˈtrəʊlə(r)/ **68**/5
airline ticket /ˈeəlaɪn tɪkɪt/ **67**/2
airmail /ˈeəmeɪl/ **32**/17
airport /ˈeəpɔːt/ **67**/**68**
(air)tank /ˈeətæŋk/ **77**/22
aisle /aɪl/ **76**/27
Alabama /ˌæləˈbæmə/ **55**
alarm clock /əˈlɑːm klɒk/ **18**/14
Alaska /əˈlæskə/ **55**
Albania /ælˈbeɪniə/ **54**
Albuquerque /ˈælbəˌkɜːrkɪ/ **55**
Algeria /ælˈdʒɪəriə/ **54**
alligator clip /ˈæligeɪtər klɪp/ **46**/7
almond /ˈɑːmənd/ **28**/17
along /əˈlɒŋ/ **57**/12
am (US A.M.) /eɪˈem/ **37**/15
AM/FM /ˌeɪ em, ˌef em/ **30**/8
ambulance /ˈæmbjʊləns/ **38**/14
ambulance service /ˈæmbjʊləns sɜːvɪs/ **38**
America /əˈmerɪkə/ **53**, **55**
American /əˈmerɪkən/ **32**, 33, 35
American football /əmerɪkən ˈfʊtbɔːl/ **78**/11
amplifier /ˈæmplɪfaɪə(r)/ **30**/16
anchor /ˈæŋkə(r)/ **70**/16
Anchorage /ˈæŋkərɪdʒ/ **55**
angler /ˈæŋglə(r)/ **72**/14
Anglesey /ˈæŋglsɪ/ **56**
Angola /æŋˈgəʊlə/ **54**
Angus /ˈæŋgəs/ **56**
animal /ˈænɪml/ **89**/**90**
ankle /ˈæŋkl/ **3**/16, **6**/14
answering machine /ˈɑːnsərɪŋ (US ˈænsərɪŋ) məˌʃiːn/ **44**/5
answerphone /ˈɑːnsəfəʊn; US ˈænsər/ **44**/5
ant /ænt/ **92**/15
Antarctic /æntˈɑːktɪk/ **53**/11
Antarctica /æntˈɑːktɪkə/ **53**/7

antenna /ænˈtenə/ **14**/20, **92**/10
antler /ˈæntlə(r)/ **90**/2
Antrim /ˈæntrɪm/ **56**
apartment house /əˈpɑːrtmənt ˌhaʊs/ **13**/10
apex /ˈeɪpeks/ **47**/1
Appalachian Mountains /æpəˌleɪʃn ˈmaʊntnz/ **55**
appetizer /ˈæpɪtaɪzə(r)/ **28**
apple /ˈæpl/ **24**/4
apple pie /æpl ˈpaɪ/ **28**/8
appointment /əˈpɔɪntmənt/ **43**/8
appointment book /əˈpɔɪntmənt bʊk/ **44**/21
April /ˈeɪprəl/ **52**
Arabian Sea /əˌreɪbiən ˈsiː/ **54**/29
arc /ɑːk/ **47**/7
arch /ɑːtʃ/ **14**/10
architect /ˈɑːkɪtekt/ **40**/1
Arctic /ˈɑːktɪk/ **53**/8
Ards /ɑːdz/ **56**
area code /ˈeərɪə kəʊd/ **38**/20
Argentina /ˌɑːdʒənˈtiːnə/ **53**
Argyll and Bute /ɑːˈgaɪl ənd ˈbjuːt/ **56**
Arizona /ˌærɪˈzəʊnə/ **55**
Arkansas /ˈɑːrkənsɔː/ **55**
arm /ɑːm/ **3**/7
Armagh /ɑːˈmɑː/ **56**
armchair /ˈɑːmtʃeə(r)/ **16**/22
Armenia /ɑːˈmiːniə/ **54**
around /əˈraʊnd/ **58**/2
arrangement /əˈreɪndʒmənt/ **25**/10
artist /ˈɑːtɪst/ **39**/1
Asia /ˈeɪʃə/ **53**/5
asparagus /əˈspærəgəs/ **23**/5
astronaut /ˈæstrənɔːt/ **50**/6
at the bottom of /æt ðə ˈbɒtəm əv/ **58**/14
at the top of /æt ðə ˈtɒp əv/ **58**/12
athlete /ˈæθliːt/ **80**/20
athletics /æθˈletɪks/ **80**/15
Atlanta /ətˈlæntə/ **55**
Atlantic /ətˈlæntɪk/ **53**
aubergine /ˈəʊbəʒiːn/ **23**/20
audience /ˈɔːdiəns/ **76**/28
August /ˈɔːgəst/ **52**
aunt /ɑːnt; US ænt/ **1**/3
Austin /ˈɒstɪn/ **55**
Australia /ɒˈstreɪliə; US ɔːˈstreɪljə/ **53**/6
Austria /ˈɒstriə/ **54**
auto racing /ˈɔːtəʊ ˌreɪsɪŋ/ **80**/5
automatic teller /ˌɔːtəmætɪk ˈtelər/ **34**/16
autumn /ˈɔːtəm/ **52**/11
avocado /ˌævəˈkɑːdəʊ/ **24**/13
away from /əˈweɪ frɒm/ **57**/9
Ayrshire /ˈeəʃə(r)/ **56**
Azerbaijan /ˌæzəbaɪˈdʒɑːn/ **54**

baby /ˈbeɪbi/ **5**/1
baby carriage /ˈbeɪbi kærɪdʒ/ **60**/3
back /bæk/ **3**/9, **48**/10
back garden /bæk ˈgɑːdn/ **22**/1
back teeth /ˌbæk ˈtiːθ/ **8**/12
backbone /ˈbækbəʊn/ **4**/14
backgammon /ˈbækgæmən/ **74**/24
backhoe /ˈbækhəʊ/ **61**/18
backpack /ˈbækpæk/ **66**/16, **71**/25
backward /ˈbækwəd/ **82**/20
backwards /ˈbækwədz/ **82**/20
backyard /ˌbækˈjɑːrd/ **22**/1
bad /bæd/ **88**/6
badminton /ˈbædmɪntən/ **78**/24

bag /bæg/ **24**/12, **26**/10, 16, **66**/13, **83**/6
baggage reclaim /ˌbægɪdʒ rɪˈkleɪm/ **67**/16
Bahamas /bəˈhɑːməz/ **53**
Bahrain /bɑːˈreɪn/ **54**
baked potato /ˌbeɪkt pəˈteɪtəʊ/ **28**/25
baker /ˈbeɪkə(r)/ **39**/7
balance /ˈbæləns/ **46**/23
balcony /ˈbælkəni/ **13**/12, **57**/14, **76**/21, 22
bald /bɔːld/ **5**/7
ball /bɔːl/ **26**/2, **78**/19
ballboy /ˈbɔːlbɔɪ/ **81**/9
ballooning /bəˈluːnɪŋ/ **72**/20
Ballymena /ˌbæliˈmiːnə/ **56**
Ballymoney /ˌbæliˈmʌni/ **56**
Baltic Sea /ˌbɔːltɪk ˈsiː/ **54**/22
Baltimore /ˈbɒltɪmɔːr/ **55**
banana /bəˈnɑːnə; US bəˈnænə/ **24**/3
Banbridge /ˈbænbrɪdʒ/ **56**
Band-Aid /ˈbændeɪd/ **7**/3
bandage /ˈbændɪdʒ/ **7**/2
Bangladesh /ˌbæŋgləˈdeʃ/ **54**
bangs /bæŋz/ **5**/14
bank /bæŋk/ **34**, **60**/18, **62**/13
(bank) account number /bæŋk əˈkaʊnt ˌnʌmbə(r)/ **34**/7
(bank) balance /bæŋk ˈbæləns/ **34**/6
bank statement /ˈbæŋk steɪtmənt/ **34**/5
bar /bɑː(r)/ **17**/8, **26**/11, **86**/20
barbecue /ˈbɑːbɪkjuː/ **22**/16
Barents Sea /ˌbɑːrənts ˈsiː/ **54**/41
barge /bɑːdʒ/ **69**/2
bark /bɑːk/ **25**/8
barn /bɑːn/ **73**/22
barrier /ˈbæriə(r)/ **66**/22
base /beɪs/ **47**/16
baseball /ˈbeɪsbɔːl/ **78**/1
baseball glove /ˈbeɪsbɔːl glʌv/ **78**/4
baseball mitt /ˈbeɪsbɔːl mɪt/ **78**/4
baseline /ˈbeɪslaɪn/ **81**/1
basement window /ˈbeɪsmənt wɪndəʊ/ **13**/9
basin /ˈbeɪsn/ **8**/5
basket /ˈbɑːskɪt; US ˈbæskɪt/ **24**/2, 22, **25**/6, **58**/2
basketball /ˈbɑːskɪtbɔːl/ **78**/8
bassoon /bəˈsuːn/ **75**/15
bat /bæt/ **78**/27, **89**/4
bath /bɑːθ; US bæθ/ **17**/15
bath-towel /ˈbɑːθtaʊəl/ **17**/11
bathing suit /ˈbeɪðɪŋ suːt/ **11**/1, 2
bathroom /ˈbɑːθruːm, rʊm; US ˈbæθruːm, rʊm/ **17**
bathroom cabinet /ˌbɑːθruːm, rʊm ˈkæbɪnɪt/ **17**/1
bathtub /ˈbæθtʌb/ **17**/15
baton /ˈbætn, ˈbætɒn; US bəˈtɒn/ **76**/5
batsman /ˈbætsmən/ **81**/14
batter /ˈbætə(r)/ **78**/3
battery /ˈbætəri/ **46**/14
batting helmet /ˈbætɪŋ helmɪt/ **78**/2
bay /beɪ/ **54**
Bay of Bengal /ˌbeɪ əv beŋˈgɔːl/ **54**/30
bay window /ˌbeɪ ˈwɪndəʊ/ **14**/11
be (verb) /biː/ **6**/1–3
beach /biːtʃ/ **72**/1, 3, **73**/10
beak /biːk/ **93**/9
bear /beə(r)/ **90**/4
beard /bɪəd/ **4**/24
Beaufort Sea /ˌbəʊfət ˈsiː/ **53**/15
bed /bed/ **18**/3, **41**/2, **42**/24
bed-linen /ˈbedlɪnɪn/ **18**/2

Bedfordshire /ˈbedfədʃə(r)/ 56
bedroom /ˈbedruːm, rʊm/ 18
bedside cabinet /ˌbedsaɪd ˈkæbɪnɪt/ 18/10
bedspread /ˈbedspred/ 18/4
bee /biː/ 92/2
beet /biːt/ 23/8
beetle /ˈbiːtl/ 92/13
beetroot /ˈbiːtruːt/ 23/8
behind /bɪˈhaɪnd/ 58/19
Belarus /ˈbelərʊs/ 54
Belfast /ˈbelfɑːst/ 56
Belgium /ˈbeldʒəm/ 54
Belize /beˈliːz/ 53
bell /bel/ 65/18
bellhop /ˈbelhɒp/ 71/2
below /bɪˈləʊ/ 52/8, 58/16
belt /belt/ 12/11
bench /bentʃ/ 22/14
bend over (verb)/ bend ˈəʊvə(r)/ 82/22
bend to right /ˌbend tʊ ˈraɪt/ 61/8
Benin /ˈbenɪn/ 54
Bering Sea /ˌberɪŋ ˈsiː/ 54/38
Berkeley /ˈbɜːrklɪ/ 55
Berkshire /ˈbɑːkʃə(r)/ 56
Bermuda /bəˈmjuːdə/ 53
beside /bɪˈsaɪd/ 58/17
between /bɪˈtwiːn/ 58/8
Bhutan /buːˈtɑːn/ 54
bicycle /ˈbaɪsɪkl/ 65/1
bicyclist /ˈbaɪsɪklɪst/ 60/20
big /bɪɡ/ 87/3
bike /baɪk/ 65, 65/1
bike and pedestrian path /baɪk ənd
  pəˈdestrɪən pæθ/ 61/9
bill /bɪl/ 35/6, 93/26
Billings /ˈbɪlɪŋz/ 55
bin /bɪn/ 57/4
binoculars /bɪˈnɒkjʊləz/ 29/7
bird /bɜːd/ 93
Birmingham /ˈbɜːrmɪŋhæm/ 55
Birmingham /ˈbɜːmɪŋəm/ 56
biscuit /ˈbɪskɪt/ 27/15, 16
biscuit tin /ˈbɪskɪt tɪn/ 16/10
Bismarck /ˈbɪzmɑːk/ 55
black /blæk/ 9/13
black and white print /ˌblæk ənd waɪt ˈprɪnt/
  29/14
black eye /blæk ˈaɪ/ 6/20
Black Sea /ˌblæk ˈsiː/ 54/26
blackboard /ˈblækbɔːd/ 49/1
Blaenau Gwent /ˌblaɪnaɪ ˈɡwent/ 56
blanket /ˈblæŋkɪt/ 18/5
blazer /ˈbleɪzə(r)/ 10/3
blind /blaɪnd/ 17/19
block of flats /blɒk əv ˈflæts/ 13/10
blonde /blɒnd/ 5/15
blood /blʌd/ 6/19
blood pressure gauge /ˈblʌd preʃə ˌɡeɪdʒ/ 7/23
blouse /blaʊz; US blaʊs/ 10/9
blow (verb) /bləʊ/ 82/23
blue /bluː/ 9/7
board /bɔːd/ 74/25
boarding /ˈbɔːdɪŋ/ 68/1
boarding pass /ˈbɔːdɪŋ pɑːs; US pæs/ 67/3
boat /bəʊt/ 60/11
boating /ˈbəʊtɪŋ/ 72/11
boil (verb) /bɔɪl/ 83/10
boiled potatoes /ˌbɔɪld pəˈteɪtəʊz/ 28/26
Bolivia /bəˈlɪvɪə/ 53

bolt /bəʊlt/ 21/24
bongos /ˈbɒŋɡəʊz/ 75/20
bonnet /ˈbɒnɪt/ 64/14
bonsai /ˈbɒnsaɪ; US also bəʊnˈsaɪ/ 25/12
book /bʊk/ 31/20, 58/4, 14, 15, 85/12
bookcase /ˈbʊkkeɪs/ 58/11–14
boot /buːt/ 10/13, 64/9
Bosnia-Herzegovina
  /ˌbɒznɪə ˌhɜːtsəɡəˈviːnə/ 54
Boston /ˈbɒstən/ 55
Botswana /bɒtˈswɑːnə/ 54
bottle /ˈbɒtl/ 27/25
bottom /ˈbɒtəm/ 3/11, 48/8
bounce (verb) /baʊns/ 82/8
boundary /ˈbaʊndrɪ/ 53, 56
bow /baʊ/ 69/16
bow /bəʊ/ 75/2
bowl (verb) /bəʊl/ 81/18
bowl /bəʊl/ 15/13
bowler /ˈbəʊlə(r)/ 81/17
bowling /ˈbəʊlɪŋ/ 79/8
bowling-alley /ˈbəʊlɪŋ ælɪ/ 79/9
box /bɒks/ 18/9, 26/9, 27/1
boxer /ˈbɒksə(r)/ 12/9
boxing /ˈbɒksɪŋ/ 79/17
boxing glove /ˈbɒksɪŋ ɡlʌv/ 79/21
boy /bɔɪ/ 5/2
bra /brɑː/ 11/9
brace /breɪs/ 21/15
bracelet /ˈbreɪslɪt/ 12/23
Bradford /ˈbrædfəd/ 56
braid /breɪd/ 5/17
brake lever /ˈbreɪk liːvə(r)/ 65/16
branch /brɑːntʃ; US bræntʃ/ 25/7
brass /brɑːs; US bræs/ 75
Brazil /brəˈzɪl/ 53
bread /bred/ 27/2
breadboard /ˈbredbɔːd/ 20/18
break (verb) /breɪk/ 6/13, 86/20
breakfast /ˈbrekfəst/ 41/9
breastbone /ˈbrestbəʊn/ 4/12
brick /brɪk/ 13/7, 16
bricklayer /ˈbrɪkleɪə(r)/ 40/12
bridge /brɪdʒ/ 8/17, 60/15
Bridgend /ˌbrɪdʒˈend/ 56
briefcase /ˈbriːfkeɪs/ 10/12
bright /braɪt/ 51/13
Brighton /ˈbraɪtn/ 56
Bristol /ˈbrɪstl/ 56
Britain /ˈbrɪtn/ 56
British /ˈbrɪtɪʃ/ 32, 33, 36
British Isles /ˌbrɪtɪʃ ˈaɪls/ 56
broccoli /ˈbrɒkəlɪ/ 23/17
brooch /brəʊtʃ/ 12/22
broom /bruːm/ 22/11
brother-in-law /ˈbrʌðər ɪn lɔː/ 1/10
brown /braʊn/ 9/4
bruise /bruːz/ 6/15
Brunei /bruːnaɪ/ 54
brush (verb) /brʌʃ/ 84/16
brush /brʌʃ/ 19/5
Brussels sprout (US brussels sprout) /ˌbrʌslz
  ˈspraʊt/ 23/15
bucket /ˈbʌkɪt/ 19/6
Buckinghamshire /ˈbʌkɪŋəmʃə(r)/ 56
buckle /ˈbʌkl/ 11/19
bud /bʌd/ 25/27
budgerigar /ˈbʌdʒərɪɡɑː(r)/ 93/20
Buffalo /ˈbʌfələʊ/ 55

buffalo /ˈbʌfələʊ/ 90/19
buffet /bəˈfeɪ/ 15/18
building /ˈbɪldɪŋ/ 13/14, 60/1
building material /ˈbɪldɪŋ məˌtɪərɪəl/ 13
built-in flash /ˌbɪltɪn ˈflæʃ/ 29/20
bulb /bʌlb/ 25/13
Bulgaria /bʌlˈɡeərɪə/ 54
bull /bʊl/ 89/3
bulletin board /ˈbʊlətɪn bɔːd/ 44/1
bumper /ˈbʌmpə(r)/ 64/7
bunch /bʌntʃ/ 24/3, 24/10, 25/9
bungalow /ˈbʌŋɡələʊ/ 14/19
Bunsen burner /ˌbʌnsn ˈbɜːnə(r)/ 45/5
bureau /ˈbjʊˈrəʊ/ 18/19
burette /bjʊəˈret/ 46/25
Burkina /bɜːˈkiːnə/ 54
Burma /ˈbɜːmə/ 54
burn (verb) /bɜːn/ 86/24
burner /ˈbɜːnə(r)/ 20/27
Burundi /bʊˈrʊndɪ/ 54
bus /bʌs/ 63/2
bus shelter /ˈbʌs ʃeltə(r)/ 59/21
bus stop /ˈbʌs stɒp/ 59/22
bush /bʊʃ/ 22/9, 58/1
butcher /ˈbʊtʃə(r)/ 39/8
butter /ˈbʌtə(r)/ 27/29
butterfly /ˈbʌtəflaɪ/ 92/6
buttocks /ˈbʌtəks/ 3/11
button /ˈbʌtən/ 74/15
buy (verb) /baɪ/ 41/11
by /baɪ/ 58/6

cab /kæb/ 60/6
cabbage /ˈkæbɪdʒ/ 23/21
cabin /ˈkæbɪn/ 69/5
cabin cruiser /ˈkæbɪn ˌkruːzə(r)/ 69/13
cabinet /ˈkæbɪnɪt/ 17/1, 18/10, 20/20
cable /ˈkeɪbl/ 65/15, 69/6
cactus /ˈkæktəs/ 25/21
caddy /ˈkædɪ/ 79/12
Caernarfonshire and Merionethshire
  /kəˈnɑːvənʃər ənd ˌmeriˈɒnəθʃə(r)/ 56
Caerphilly /kəˈfɪlɪ/ 56
café /ˈkæfeɪ; US kæˈfeɪ/ 59/4
cake /keɪk/ 28/13
calculator /ˈkælkjʊleɪtə(r)/ 49/5
calendar /ˈkælɪndə(r)/ 44/2
calf /kɑːf; US kæf/ 89/2
California /ˌkælɪˈfɔːnɪə/ 55
Cambodia /kæmˈbəʊdɪə/ 54
Cambridge /ˈkeɪmbrɪdʒ/ 56
Cambridgeshire /ˈkeɪmbrɪdʒʃə(r)/ 56
camcorder /ˈkæmkɔːdə(r)/ 30/1
camel /ˈkæml/ 90/10
camera /ˈkæmərə/ 29/16, 19, 23
camera case /ˈkæmərə keɪs/ 29/21
camera shop /ˈkæmərə ʃɒp/ 29
camera store /ˈkæmərə stɔːr/ 29
Cameroon /ˌkæməˈruːn/ 54
camp stove /ˈkæmp stəʊv/ 71/22
camping /ˈkæmpɪŋ/ 71/18
camping stove /ˈkæmpɪŋ stəʊv/ 71/22
can /kæn/ 27/6, 26
can opener /ˈkæn əʊpənər/ 20/10
Canada /ˈkænədə/ 53
canal /kəˈnæl/ 72/12
canary /kəˈneərɪ/ 93/18
Canary Islands /kəˈneərɪ ˌaɪləndz/ 54
candle /ˈkændl/ 15/3, 58/8, 9, 86/23, 24

candy /'kændɪ/ **26**/10, 14, 15, 18
canoe /kə'nuː/ **69**/19
cap /kæp/ **10**/2
capacity /kə'pæsəti/ **48**/26
capital city /,kæpɪtl 'sɪti/ **56**
capsule /'kæpsjuːl; US 'kæpsl/ **7**/6
car /kɑː(r)/ **60**/24, **64**
car accident /'kɑːr ,æksɪdənt/ **38**/13
car-park /'kɑːpɑːk/ **13**/15
caravan /'kærəvæn/ **63**/9, **71**/27
caravan site /'kærəvæn saɪt/ **71**/26
card file /'kɑːd faɪl/ **44**/8
card index /'kɑːd ɪndeks/ **44**/8
Cardiff /'kɑːdɪf/ **56**
cardigan /'kɑːdɪgən/ **12**/7
Cardiganshire /'kɑːdɪgənʃə(r)/ **56**
cargo /'kɑːgəʊ/ **70**/4
Caribbean Sea /,kærɪ,biːən 'siː/ **53**/19
Carlow /'kɑːləʊ/ **56**
Carmarthenshire /kə'mɑːðənʃə(r)/ **56**
carnation /kɑː'neɪʃn/ **25**/24
Carolina /kærə'laɪnə/ **55**
carpenter /'kɑːpəntə(r)/ **40**/8
carpet /'kɑːpɪt/ **16**/7
Carrickfergus /,kærɪk'fɜːgəs/ **56**
carrot /'kærət/ **23**/14
carry (verb) /'kæri/ **86**/14
cart /kɑːt/ **28**/6, **46**/15, **67**/18, **68**/3, **86**/21
carton /'kɑːtən/ **27**/21
cash (verb) /kæʃ/ **34**/10, 14
cash /kæʃ/ **34**/15, 35
cash dispenser /'kæʃ dɪspensə(r)/ **34**/16
cash machine /'kæʃ məʃiːn/ **34**/16
cash register /'kæʃ ,redʒɪstə(r)/ **29**/3
cashier /kæ'ʃɪə(r)/ **34**/9
cashpoint /'kæʃpɔɪnt/ **34**/16
Caspian Sea /,kæspiən 'siː/ **54**/27
casserole /'kæsərəʊl/ **20**/1
cassette /kə'set/ **30**/6, **58**/3
cassette deck /kə'set dek/ **30**/18
cast /kæst/ **7**/13
castle /'kɑːsl; US 'kæsl/ **71**/13
Castlereagh /'kɑːslreɪ/ **56**
cat /kæt/ **89**/18
catch (verb) /kætʃ/ **42**/13, **82**/10
catcher /'kætʃə(r)/ **78**/6
catcher's mask /'kætʃərz mæsk/ **78**/5
caterpillar /'kætəpɪlə(r)/ **92**/8
cauliflower /'kɒlɪflaʊə(r); US 'kɔːli-/ **23**/4
Cavan /'kævən/ **56**
CD /,siː 'diː/ **30**/7
CD player /,siː 'diː ,pleɪə(r)/ **30**/19
ceiling /'siːlɪŋ/ **16**/1
celery /'seləri/ **23**/16
cello /'tʃeləʊ/ **75**/3
Celsius /'selsiəs/ **52**/2
cement truck /sɪ'ment trʌk/ **63**/6
cement-mixer /sɪ'mentmɪksə(r)/ **63**/6
cent /sent/ **35**/13
center /'sentər/ **47**/4
center lane /'sentər leɪn/ **62**/16
centigrade /'sentigreɪd/ **52**/2
centimetre /'sentɪmiːtə(r)/ **48**/30
Central African Republic /,sentrəl ,æfrɪkən rɪ'pʌblɪk/ **54**
central reservation /,sentrəl rezə'veɪʃn/ **62**/8
centre /'sentə(r)/ **47**/4
centre lane /'sentə leɪn/ **62**/6
century /'sentʃəri/ **37**

cereal /'sɪəriəl/ **27**/1
certified mail /,sɜːtɪfaɪd 'meɪl/ **32**/21
Chad /tʃæd/ **54**
chain /tʃeɪn/ **12**/25, **65**/8
chain-wheel /tʃeɪnwiːl; US also hwiːl/ **65**/10
chair /tʃeə(r)/ **49**/10
chalk /tʃɔːk/ **49**/24
chalkboard /'tʃɔːkbɔːd/ **49**/1
change (verb) /tʃeɪndʒ/ **34**/10, 12, **35**/16
Charleston /'tʃɑːlstən/ **55**
Charlotte /ʃɑːlət/ **55**
cheap /tʃiːp/ **87**/7
check /tʃek/ **9**/19
check-in /'tʃekɪn/ **67**/1
check-in counter /'tʃekɪn ,kaʊntər/ **67**/4
check-in desk /'tʃekɪn ,desk/ **67**/4
checked /tʃekt/ **9**/19
checkers /'tʃekərz/ **74**/26
cheek /tʃiːk/ **4**/19
cheese /tʃiːz/ **27**/22
cheesecake /'tʃiːzkeɪk/ **28**/9
cheque (US check) /tʃek/ **34**/14, **43**/4
cheque book (US checkbook) /'tʃek bʊk/ **34**/1
cheque card /'tʃek kɑːd/ **34**/3
cheque stub (US check stub) /'tʃek stʌb/ **34**/2
cherry /'tʃeri/ **28**/1
Cheshire /'tʃeʃə(r)/ **56**
chess /tʃes/ **74**/29
chest /tʃest/ **3**/26
chest of drawers /'tʃest əv drɔːz/ **18**/19
Chicago /ʃɪ'kɑːgəʊ/ **55**
chick /tʃɪk/ **93**/3
chicken /'tʃɪkɪn/ **27**/10, **93**/1
child /tʃaɪld/ **5**/2, **85**/2–4
children /'tʃɪldrən/ **1**/19
Chile /'tʃɪli/ **53**
chimney /'tʃɪmni/ **14**/7
chin /tʃɪn/ **3**/28
China /'tʃaɪnə/ **54**
chips /tʃɪps/ **28**/27
chisel /'tʃɪzl/ **21**/14
chocolate /'tʃɒklət/ **26**/9, 11, 17, **28**/13
chop (verb) /tʃɒp/ **79**/28
Christmas tree /'krɪsməs triː/ **25**/1
chrysanthemum /krɪ'sænθəməm/ **25**/15
Cincinnati /,sɪnsɪ'næti/ **55**
cinema /'sɪnəmɑː, 'sɪnəmə/ **76**
circle /'sɜːkl/ **47**/1, **76**/21
circumference /sə'kʌmfərəns/ **47**/2
city /'sɪti/ **55, 56, 59**/60
Clackmannanshire /klæk'mænənʃə(r)/ **56**
clamp stand /'klæmp stænd/ **45**/20
clap (verb) /klæp/ **85**/8
Clare /kleə(r)/ **56**
clarinet /'klærɪ'net/ **75**/14
classroom /'klɑːsruːm, rʊm; US 'klæs-/ **49**
claw /klɔː/ **90**/5, **91**/19
clean (verb) /kliːn/ **83**/3
clean /kliːn/ **88**/19
Cleveland /'kliːvlənd/ **55**
cliff /klɪf/ **73**/11
climb (verb) /klaɪm/ **82**/13
climber /'klaɪmə(r)/ **72**/25
climbing /'klaɪmɪŋ/ **72**/24
clock /klɒk/ **15**/26, **58**/8
clock-face /'klɒkfeɪs/ **37**/2
closed /kləʊzd/ **87**/10
closet /'klɒzɪt/ **18**/17
clothes /kləʊðz; US kləʊz/ **9**/11

clothes-line /'kləʊðzlaɪn; US 'kləʊz-/ **19**/22
clothes-peg /'kləʊðzpeg/ **19**/10
clothespin /'kləʊzpɪn/ **19**/10
cloudy /'klaʊdi/ **51**/8
club /klʌb/ **74**/31, **79**/15
clutch /klʌtʃ/ **64**/26
coach /kəʊtʃ/ **63**/2, **66**/4
coat /kəʊt/ **10**/17
coat-hanger /'kəʊthæŋə(r)/ **18**/18
(cob)web /'kɒbweb/ **92**/12
cock /kɒk/ **93**/4
cockpit /'kɒkpɪt/ **68**/14
cockroach /'kɒkrəʊtʃ/ **92**/16
cocktail /'kɒkteɪl/ **28**/11
coconut /'kəʊkənʌt/ **24**/7
cocoon /kə'kuːn/ **92**/7
coffee-pot /'kɒfɪ,pɒt; US 'kɔːfɪ,pɒt/ **15**/21
coffee-table /'kɒfɪ,teɪbl; US 'kɔːfɪ-/ **16**/8
coin /kɔɪn/ **35**/1, **36**/1
colander /'kʌləndə(r)/ **20**/9
cold /kəʊld/ **6**/7, **52**/6
cold water faucet /'kəʊld wɔːtər ,fɔːsɪt/ **19**/19
cold(-water) tap /'kəʊld'wɔːtə ,tæp/ **19**/19
Coleraine /'kəʊlə,reɪn/ **56**
collar /'kɒlə(r)/ **11**/15
collection /kə'lekʃn/ **31**/6
Colombia /kə'lʌmbiə/ **53**
Colorado /,kɒlə'rɑːdəʊ/ **55**
colour (US color) /'kʌlə(r)/ **9**
colour print (US color print) /'kʌlə prɪnt/ **29**/13
coloured pens (US colored pens) /'kʌləd penz/ **26**/5
Columbia /kə'lʌmbiə/ **55**
comb (verb) /kəʊm/ **84**/15
comb /kəʊm/ **17**/27
combine harvester (US combine) /,kɒmbaɪn 'hɑːvɪstə(r)/ **73**/25
come (verb) /kʌm/ **57**/7
come back (verb) /kʌm 'bæk/ **41**/5
compact camera /,kɒmpækt 'kæmərə/ **29**/19
compact disc /,kɒmpækt 'dɪsk/ **30**/7
compact disc player /,kɒmpækt 'dɪsk ,pleɪə(r)/ **30**/19
compass /'kʌmpəs/ **49**/19
compasses /'kʌmpəsɪz/ **49**/19
computer programmer /kəm'pjuːtə ,prəʊgræmə(r)/ **40**/5
concrete /'kɒŋkriːt/ **13**/18
concrete wall /,kɒŋkriːt 'wɔːl/ **14**/12
condenser /kən'densə(r)/ **45**/23
conductor /kən'dʌktə(r)/ **76**/4
cone /kəʊn/ **47**/22, **61**/17
confectionery /kən'fekʃənəri/ **26**
conga /'kɒŋgə/ **75**/22
Congo /'kɒŋgəʊ/ **54**
conical flask /'kɒnɪkl flɑːsk; US flæsk/ **45**/17
Connecticut /kə'netɪkət/ **55**
constellation /,kɒnstə'leɪʃn/ **50**/25
construction worker /kən'strʌkʃn ,wɜːkə(r)/ **61**/15
contact lens /,kɒntækt 'lenz/ **8**/20
contact lens cleaner /,kɒntækt 'lenz kliːnə(r)/ **8**/22
container /kən'teɪnər/ **27**/19
continent /'kɒntɪnənt/ **53**
contrastive adjective /kən'trɑːstɪv ,ædʒɪktɪv/ **87**/88

control tower /kənˈtrəʊl taʊə(r)/ **68**/4
convertible /kənˈvɜːtəbl/ **63**/13
cook (verb) /kʊk/ **83**/2
cookbook /ˈkʊkbʊk/ **20**/4
cooked meat /ˌkʊkd ˈmiːt/ **27**/7
cookery book /ˈkʊkəri bʊk/ **20**/4
cookie /ˈkʊki/ **27**/15, 16
cookie tin /ˈkʊki tɪn/ **16**/10
Cookstown /ˈkʊksˌtaʊn/ **56**
cool /kuːl/ **52**/5
coping saw /ˈkəʊpɪŋ ˌsɔː/ **21**/20
copy /ˈkɒpi/ **43**/11
Coral Sea /ˌkɒrəl ˈsiː/ **54**/32
cord /kɔːd/ **19**/11
Cork /kɔːk/ **56**
corn /kɔːn/ **28**/20
corner /ˈkɔːnə(r)/ **48**/5, **79**/18
cornfield /ˈkɔːnfiːld/ **73**/26
Cornwall /ˈkɔːnwəl/ **56**
correction fluid /kəˈrekʃn fluːɪd/ **44**/9
Costa Rica /ˌkɒstə ˈriːkə/ **53**
Côte d'Ivoire /ˌkəʊt diːˈvwɑː/ **54**
cottage /ˈkɒtɪdʒ/ **14**/13
cotton /ˈkɒtn/ **74**/11
cotton ball /ˈkɒtn bɔːl/ **7**/4
cotton wool /ˈkɒtn ˈwʊl/ **7**/4
couch /kaʊtʃ/ **16**/17
cough /kɒf; US kɔːf/ **6**/9
counter /ˈkaʊntə(r)/ **20**/13, **31**/3
counter assistant /ˌkaʊntər əˈsɪstənt/ **31**/4
counterfoil /ˈkaʊntəfɔɪl/ **34**/2
country /ˈkʌntri/ **53**, **56**
country code /ˈkʌntri kəʊd/ **38**/19
country house /ˌkʌntri ˈhaʊs/ **71**/14
countryside /ˈkʌntrisaɪd/ **71**/16
county /ˈkaʊnti/ **56**
courgette /kɔːˈʒet/ **23**/12
courier /ˈkʊriə(r)/ **31**/15
courtyard /ˈkɔːtjɑːd/ **57**/2
cousin /ˈkʌzn/ **1**/9
Coventry /ˈkɒvəntri/ **56**
cow /kaʊ/ **89**/1
crab /kræb/ **91**/18
Craigavon /kreɪgˈævən/ **56**
crane /kreɪn/ **70**/2
crank /kræŋk/ **65**/5
crash barrier /ˈkræʃ bæriə(r)/ **62**/9
cream /kriːm/ **9**/6, **28**/12
credit card /ˈkredɪt kɑːd/ **34**/4
crescent /ˈkresnt/ **50**/1
cricket /ˈkrɪkɪt/ **81**, **92**/18
cricket match /ˈkrɪkɪt mætʃ/ **81**/12
crisps /krɪsps/ **26**/16, 19
Croatia /krəʊˈeɪʃə/ **54**
crocodile /ˈkrɒkədaɪl/ **91**/29
crocodile clip /ˈkrɒkədaɪl ˌklɪp/ **46**/7
crooked /ˈkrʊkɪd/ **87**/2
crossroads /ˈkrɒsrəʊds/ **60**/21
crosswalk /ˈkrɒswɔːk/ **59**/24
crow /krəʊ/ **93**/11
crowd /kraʊd/ **78**/7
crucible /ˈkruːsɪbl/ **46**/26
cruise /kruːz/ **72**/6
crutch /krʌtʃ/ **7**/14
cry (verb) /kraɪ/ **84**/20
Cuba /ˈkjuːbə/ **53**
cube /kjuːb/ **47**/21
cucumber /ˈkjuːkʌmbə(r)/ **23**/10
cue /kjuː/ **79**/5

cuff /kʌf/ **11**/17
Cumbria /ˈkʌmbriə/ **56**
cup /kʌp/ **16**/14, **42**/16, **58**/16
cupboard /ˈkʌbəd/ **20**/20
curb /kɜːb/ **59**/9
curly /ˈkɜːli/ **5**/10
curtains /ˈkɜːtnz/ **16**/20
curve /kɜːv/ **47**/27
curve to right /ˌkɜːv tʊ ˈraɪt/ **61**/8
cushion /ˈkʊʃn/ **16**/18
customer /ˈkʌstəmə(r)/ **29**/1
customs /ˈkʌstəms/ **67**/19
customs officer /ˈkʌstəmz ˌɒfɪsə(r)/ **67**/20
cut (verb) /kʌt/ **86**/17
cut /kʌt/ **6**/18
cutting board /ˈkʌtɪŋ bɔːd/ **20**/18
cycle (verb) /ˈsaɪkl/ **80**/4
cycle and pedestrian route /ˌsaɪkl ənd pəˈdestriən ruːt/ **61**/9
cycling /ˈsaɪklɪŋ/ **80**/3
cyclist /ˈsaɪklɪst/ **60**/20
cylinder /ˈsɪlɪndə(r)/ **47**/24
cylinder head /ˈsɪlɪndə(r) hed/ **64**/17
cymbals /ˈsɪmblz/ **75**/21
Cyprus /ˈsaɪprəs/ **54**
Czech Republic /ˌtʃek rɪˈpʌblɪk/ **54**

daffodil /ˈdæfədɪl/ **25**/14
daily routine /ˌdeɪli ruːˈtiːn/ **41**/12
daisy /ˈdeɪzi/ **25**/23
Dakota /dəˈkəʊtə/ **55**
Dallas /ˈdæləs/ **55**
dam /dæm/ **73**/14
dance (verb) /dɑːns; US dæns/ **85**/7
dark /dɑːk/ **5**/8, **9**/12, **51**/14
dartboard /ˈdɑːtbɔːd/ **79**/2
darts /dɑːts/ **79**/1
dashboard /ˈdæʃbɔːd/ **64**/20
date /deɪt/ **33**
daughter /ˈdɔːtə(r)/ **1**/17
day /deɪ/ **37**
Dayton /ˈdeɪtn/ **55**
December /dɪˈsembə(r)/ **52**
deck /dek/ **69**/4
deep /diːp/ **87**/19
deer /dɪə(r)/ **90**/1
degrees /dɪˈgriːz/ **52**/1, 2, 8
Delaware /ˈdeləweə(r)/ **55**
delicatessen /ˌdelɪkəˈtesn/ **27**
delivery /dɪˈlɪvəri/ **31**/12, 15
Denbighshire /ˈdenbɪʃə(r)/ **56**
Denmark /ˈdenmɑːk/ **54**
dental assistant /ˈdentl əˌsɪstənt/ **8**/6
dental nurse /ˈdentl ˌnɜːs/ **8**/6
dentist /ˈdentɪst/ **8**/1
dentist's chair /ˈdentɪsts ˌtʃeə(r)/ **8**/4
Denver /ˈdenvə(r)/ **55**
department store /dɪˈpɑːtmənt stɔː(r)/ **59**/18
departures board /dɪˈpɑːtʃəz bɔːd/ **66**/17
departures lounge /dɪˈpɑːtʃəz ˌlaʊndʒ/ **67**/12
deposit slip /dɪˈpɒzɪt slɪp/ **34**/18
depth /depθ/ **48**/1
Derby /ˈdɑːbi/ **56**
Derbyshire /ˈdɑːbɪʃə(r)/ **56**
Des Moines /də ˈmɔɪn/ **55**
describe (verb) /dɪˈskraɪb/ **9**
description /dɪˈskrɪpʃn/ **5**
desert /ˈdezət/ **73**/15

desk /desk/ **44**/6
despatch-rider /dɪˈspætʃ raɪdə(r)/ **31**/16
dessert /dɪˈzɜːt/ **28**, **28**/6
detached house /dɪˌtætʃt ˈhaʊs/ **14**/1
detergent /dɪˈtɜːdʒənt/ **19**/1
Detroit /dɪˈtrɔɪt/ **55**
Devon /ˈdevən/ **56**
diagonal /daɪˈægənl/ **47**/12
dial /daɪəl/ **38**/8
diameter /daɪˈæmɪtə(r)/ **47**/5
diamond /ˈdaɪəmənd/ **74**/33
diary /ˈdaɪəri/ **44**/21
dice /daɪs/ **74**/28
Dictaphone /ˈdɪktəfəʊn/ **43**/2
dictate (verb) /dɪkˈteɪt/ **43**/1
dictating machine /dɪkˈteɪtɪŋ məˌʃiːn/ **43**/2
difficult /ˈdɪfɪkəlt/ **87**/12
dig (verb) /dɪg/ **83**/7
dime /daɪm/ **35**/4
dining-room /ˈdaɪnɪŋruːm, rʊm/ **15**
dinner /ˈdɪnə(r)/ **42**/22
dirty /ˈdɜːti/ **88**/20
disc jockey /ˈdɪsk dʒɒki/ **39**/3
dish /dɪʃ/ **15**/6
dish towel /ˈdɪʃ taʊəl/ **20**/7
dishwashing liquid /ˈdɪʃwɒʃɪŋ ˌlɪkwɪd/ **20**/5
disk drive /ˈdɪsk draɪv/ **44**/24
disk jockey /ˈdɪsk dʒɒki/ **39**/3
district /ˈdɪstrɪkt/ **56**
District of Columbia /ˌdɪstrɪkt əv kəˈlʌmbiə/ **55**
dive (verb) /daɪv/ **77**/29
diver /ˈdaɪvə(r)/ **77**/30
divided by /dɪˈvaɪdɪd baɪ/ **48**/14
Djibouti /dʒɪˈbuːti/ **54**
do a handstand (verb) /ˌduː ə ˈhændstænd/ **82**/25
do not enter /ˌduː nɒt ˈentə(r)/ **61**/3
dock /dɒk/ **70**/1
doctor /ˈdɒktə(r)/ **7**/19
doctor's office /ˈdɒktərz ˌɒfɪs/ **7**
doctor's surgery /ˈdɒktəz ˌsɜːdʒəri/ **7**
dog /dɒg/ **89**/22
dollar /ˈdɒlər/ **35**/12, 13
dollar bill /ˌdɒlər ˈbɪl/ **35**/7
dolphin /ˈdɒlfɪn/ **90**/29
Dominican Republic /dəˌmɪnɪkən rɪˈpʌblɪk/ **53**
Donegal /ˈdɒnɪgɔːl/ **56**
donkey /ˈdɒŋki/ **89**/11
doormat /ˈdɔːmæt/ **18**/21
doorstep /ˈdɔːstep/ **13**/6
dormer /ˈdɔːmə(r)/ **14**/15
Dorset /ˈdɔːsɪt/ **56**
double room /ˌdʌbl ˈruːm, rʊm/ **71**/7
double yellow lines /ˌdʌbl ˌjeləʊ ˈlaɪnz/ **60**/22
(double-)bass /ˌdʌblˈbeɪs/ **75**/5
double-decker bus /ˌdʌblˌdekə ˈbʌs/ **60**/25
doubles match /ˈdʌblz mætʃ/ **81**/8
Douglas /ˈdʌgləs/ **56**
Dover /ˈdəʊvə(r)/ **56**
Down /daʊn/ **56**
down /daʊn/ **57**/13
downstairs /ˌdaʊnˈsteəz/ **18**/23, **41**/3
dozen /ˈdʌzn/ **27**/13
dragonfly /ˈdrægənflaɪ/ **92**/5
drainpipe /ˈdreɪnpaɪp/ **14**/21
drapes /dreɪps/ **16**/20
draughts /drɑːfts/ **74**/26

drawer /drɔ:(r)/ **15**/19, **58**/3
drawing /ˈdrɔ:ɪŋ/ **74**/2
dress /dres/ **12**/19
dresser /ˈdresər/ **18**/1
dressing gown /ˈdresɪŋ gaʊn/ **11**/13
dressing table /ˈdresɪŋ teɪbl/ **18**/1
dressing up /ˌdresɪŋ ˈʌp/ **12**
dried flowers /draɪd ˈflaʊəz/ **25**/9, **58**/7
drill /drɪl/ **8**/2, **21**/10, 18
drink (verb) /drɪŋk/ **42**/16
drive (verb) /draɪv/ **42**/19
drive /draɪv/ **22**/26
driveway /ˈdraɪvweɪ/ **22**/26
dropper /ˈdrɒpə(r)/ **46**/11
drum /drʌm/ **76**/10
drummer /ˈdrʌmə(r)/ **76**/11
drumsticks /ˈdrʌmstɪks/ **75**/19
dry (verb) /draɪ/ **84**/14
dry /draɪ/ **88**/9
Dublin /ˈdʌblɪn/ **56**
duck /dʌk/ **93**/28
dull /dʌl/ **51**/14
Dumbarton and Clydebank /dʌmˈbɑ:tən ənd ˈklaɪdbæŋk/ **56**
Dumfries and Galloway /dʌmˌfri:s ənd ˈɡæləweɪ/ **56**
dump truck /ˈdʌmp trʌk/ **61**/14
dumper (truck) /ˈdʌmpə ˌtrʌk/ **61**/14
Dundee /dʌnˈdi:/ **56**
Dungannon /dʌŋˈɡænən/ **56**
Durham /ˈdʌrəm/ **56**
dust cloth /ˈdʌst klɒθ/ **19**/14
dustbin /ˈdʌstbɪn/ **22**/20
duster /ˈdʌstə(r)/ **19**/14
dustpan /ˈdʌstpæn/ **19**/4
duty-free shop /djuːtɪˈfri: ˌʃɒp/ **67**/10

eagle /ˈi:ɡl/ **93**/8
ear /ɪə(r)/ **3**/3
earring /ˈɪərɪŋ/ **12**/27
Earth /ɜ:θ/ **50**/21
easel /ˈi:zl/ **49**/13
east /i:st/ **56**
East China Sea /ˌi:st ˌtʃaɪnə ˈsi:/ **54**/34
East Dunbartonshire /ˌi:st dʌnˈbɑ:tənʃə(r)/ **56**
East Riding of Yorkshire /ˌi:st ˌraɪdɪŋ əv ˈjɔ:kʃə(r)/ **56**
easy /ˈi:zɪ/ **87**/11
eat (verb) /i:t/ **41**/9, **42**/17, 22
Ecuador /ˈekwədɔ:(r)/ **53**
edge /edʒ/ **48**/4
Edinburgh /ˈedɪnbərə/ **56**
eel /i:l/ **91**/11
egg /eɡ/ **27**/13, 14
eggplant /ˈeɡplænt/ **23**/20
Egypt /ˈi:dʒɪpt/ **54**
eight /eɪt/ **33**/8
eighteen /ˌeɪˈti:n/ **33**/18
eighth /eɪtθ/ **33**
eighty /ˈeɪtɪ/ **33**/80
El Paso /el ˈpæsəʊ/ **55**
El Salvador /el ˈsælvədɔ:(r)/ **53**
elbow /ˈelbəʊ/ **3**/8
elderly /ˈeldəlɪ/ **5**/6
electric drill /ɪˌlektrɪk ˈdrɪl/ **21**/10
(electric) guitar /ɪˌlektrɪk ɡɪˈtɑ:(r)/ **76**/8
electric razor /ɪˌlektrɪk ˈreɪzə(r)/ **17**/22
electric teakettle /ɪˌlektrɪk ˈti:ketl/ **20**/19

electrician /ɪˌlekˈtrɪʃn/ **40**/7
electrode /ɪˈlektrəʊd/ **46**/6
electronics store /ɪlekˈtrɒnɪks stɔ:r/ **30**
elephant /ˈelɪfənt/ **90**/24
eleven /ɪˈlevn/ **33**/11
eleventh /ɪˈlevnθ/ **33**
embankment /ɪmˈbæŋkmənt/ **62**/3
embroidery /ɪmˈbrɔɪdərɪ/ **74**/18
emergency services /ɪˈmɜ:dʒənsɪ ˌsɜ:vɪsɪz/ **38**
empty /ˈemptɪ/ **88**/12
engine /ˈendʒɪn/ **64**/15, **65**/28, **66**/3
England /ˈɪŋɡlənd/ **56**
English Channel /ˌɪŋɡlɪʃ ˈtʃænl/ **56**
entrance /ˈentrəns/ **66**/21
envelope /ˈenvələʊp/ **26**/3, **32**/6
environment /ɪnˈvaɪərənmənt/ **73**
equals /ˈi:kwəlz/ **48**/15
equator /ɪˈkweɪtə(r)/ **53**/54
Equatorial Guinea /ekwəˌtɔ:rɪəl ˈɡɪnɪ/ **54**
eraser /ɪˈreɪzər/ **49**/26
Eritrea /ˌerɪˈtreɪə/ **54**
Essex /ˈesɪks/ **56**
estate /ɪsˈteɪt/ **63**/14
Estonia /eˈstəʊnɪə/ **54**
Ethiopia /ˌi:θɪˈəʊpɪə/ **54**
Eugene /juˈdʒi:n/ **55**
Europe /ˈjʊərəp/ **53**/4
evening /ˈi:vnɪŋ/ **37**/17
examination couch /ɪɡˌzæmɪˈneɪʃn kaʊtʃ/ **7**/22
examination table /ɪɡˌzæmɪˈneɪʃn teɪbl/ **7**/22
examining table /ɪɡˈzæmɪnɪŋ teɪbl/ **7**/22
exchange rate /ɪksˈtʃeɪndʒ reɪt/ **34**/8
exercise book /ˈeksəsaɪz bʊk/ **49**/4
exhaust-pipe /ɪɡˈzɔ:stpaɪp/ **64**/10
exit ramp /ˈeksɪt ræmp/ **62**/12
exit sign /ˈeksɪt saɪn/ **66**/5
expensive /ɪkˈspensɪv/ **87**/8
Express Mail /ɪkˈspres meɪl/ **32**/25
eye /aɪ/ **4**/25, **6**/13
eye drops /ˈaɪ drɒps/ **8**/21
eye test /ˈaɪ test/ **8**/14
eyebrow /ˈaɪbraʊ/ **4**/26
eyeglass case /ˈaɪɡlæs ˌkeɪs/ **8**/19
eyelash /ˈaɪlæʃ/ **4**/28
eyelid /ˈaɪlɪd/ **4**/27
eyepiece /ˈaɪpi:s/ **46**/22

face /feɪs/ **4**/17
face mask /ˈfeɪs mæsk/ **78**/5
factory /ˈfæktərɪ/ **59**/23
Faeroe Islands /ˈfeərəʊ ˌaɪləndz/ **54**
Fahrenheit /ˈfærənhaɪt/ **52**/1
fair /feə(r)/ **5**/9
fairway /ˈfeəweɪ/ **79**/13
Falkirk /ˈfɔ:lkɜ:k/ **56**
Falkland Islands /ˈfɔ:lklənd ˌaɪləndz/ **53**
fall (verb) /fɔ:l/ **57**/8, **82**/5
fall /fɔ:l/ **52**/11
fall over (verb) /fɔ:l ˈəʊvə(r)/ **6**/11
family relationships /ˌfæməlɪ rɪˈleɪʃnʃɪps/ **1**/2
farm /fɑ:m/ **73**/20
farmer /ˈfɑ:mə(r)/ **39**/9
farmhouse /ˈfɑ:mhaʊs/ **73**/21
fast /fɑ:st; US fæst/ **87**/23
fast lane /ˈfɑ:st leɪn; US ˈfæst/ **62**/7, 17
fat /fæt/ **5**/21
father /ˈfɑ:ðə(r)/ **1**/6
father-in-law /ˈfɑ:ðər ɪn lɔ:/ **1**/7

faucet /ˈfɔ:sɪt/ **19**/19, 20
fax (verb) /fæks/ **43**/10
fax /fæks/ **43**/10
feather /ˈfeðə(r)/ **93**/5
February /ˈfebrʊərɪ; US ˈfebrʊerɪ/ **52**
fence /fens/ **22**/15
fender /ˈfendər/ **65**/22
Fermanagh /fəˈmænə/ **56**
fern /fɜ:n/ **25**/5
ferry /ˈferɪ/ **70**/9
field /fi:ld/ **73**/24, **80**/16, **81**/22
field hockey /ˈfi:ld hɒkɪ/ **78**/16
fielder /ˈfi:ldə(r)/ **81**/21
Fife /faɪf/ **56**
fifteen /ˌfɪfˈti:n/ **33**/15
fifth /fɪfθ/ **33**
fifty /ˈfɪftɪ/ **33**/50
Fiji /ˈfi:ˌdʒi:/ **54**
file (verb) /faɪl/ **43**/9
file /faɪl/ **21**/13, **44**/14
file cabinet /ˈfaɪl ˌkæbɪnɪt/ **44**/15
filing cabinet /ˈfaɪlɪŋ ˌkæbɪnɪt/ **44**/15
fill (verb) /fɪl/ **83**/9
fill in (verb) /fɪl ˈɪn/ **43**/5
fill out (verb) /fɪl ˈaʊt/ **43**/5
filling /ˈfɪlɪŋ/ **8**/9
filling-station /ˈfɪlɪŋsteɪʃn/ **64**/1
film /fɪlm/ **29**/11
film star /ˈfɪlm stɑ:(r)/ **76**/24
filter paper /ˈfɪltə peɪpə(r)/ **45**/11
fin /fɪn/ **91**/3
finger /ˈfɪŋɡə(r)/ **3**/20
finish (verb) /ˈfɪnɪʃ/ **42**/18
Finland /ˈfɪnlənd/ **54**
fire /ˈfaɪə(r)/ **16**/4, **38**/8
fire brigade /ˈfaɪə brɪˌɡeɪd/ **38**
fire department /ˈfaɪər dɪˌpɑ:rtmənt/ **38**
fire extinguisher /ˈfaɪər ɪkˌstɪŋwɪʃə(r)/ **38**/9
fire fighter /ˈfaɪər faɪtər/ **38**/10
fire-engine /ˈfaɪərendʒɪn/ **38**/4
fireman /ˈfaɪəmən/ **38**/10
fireplace /ˈfaɪəpleɪs/ **16**/3, **58**/6, 7
first /fɜ:st/ **33**
first class mail /ˈfɜ:rst klæs ˈmeɪl/ **32**/14
first floor /ˌfɜ:rst ˈflɔ:(r)/ **13**/13, 14
first quarter /ˌfɜ:rst ˈkwɔ:rtər/ **50**/2
first-class post /ˌfɜ:stklɑ:s ˈpəʊst/ **32**/11
fish /fɪʃ/ **91**
fisherman /ˈfɪʃəmən/ **39**/10
fishing /ˈfɪʃɪŋ/ **72**/13
fishing boat /ˈfɪʃɪŋ bəʊt/ **69**/14
fishing-rod /ˈfɪʃɪŋrɒd/ **72**/15
fist /fɪst/ **3**/10
five /faɪv/ **33**/5
fizzy drink /ˌfɪzɪ ˈdrɪŋk/ **27**/26
flag /flæɡ/ **59**/19
flame /fleɪm/ **45**/3
flamingo /fləˈmɪŋɡəʊ/ **93**/25
flannel /ˈflænl/ **17**/13
flap /flæp/ **32**/7
flash (gun) /ˈflæʃ ɡʌn/ **29**/18
flashlight /ˈflæʃlaɪt/ **19**/17
flat bottom flask /ˌflæt bɒtəm ˈflɑ:sk; US flæsk/ **45**/9
flex /fleks/ **19**/11
flight attendant /flaɪt əˈtendənt/ **67**/14
Flintshire /ˈflɪntʃə(r)/ **56**
flipper /ˈflɪpə(r)/ **90**/28
floor /flɔ:(r)/ **13**/11, 13, 14, **49**/9

**floppy disk** /ˌflɒpɪ ˈdɪsk/ **44**/23
**Florida** /ˈflɒrɪdə/ **55**
**florist** /ˈflɒrɪst/ **25**
**flower** /ˈflaʊə(r)/ **57**/12
**flower-bed** /ˈflaʊəbed/ **22**/24
**flowerpot** /ˈflaʊəpɒt/ **22**/10
**flute** /fluːt/ **75**/12
**fly** /flaɪ/ **92**/1
**flyover** /ˈflaɪəʊvə(r)/ **62**/10
**foal** /fəʊl/ **89**/14
**focusing control** /ˈfəʊkəsɪŋ kənˌtrəʊl/ **46**/18
**focusing knob** /ˈfəʊkəsɪŋ nɒb/ **46**/18
**foggy** /ˈfɒgɪ/ **51**/7
**fold (verb)** /fəʊld/ **86**/19
**food processor** /ˈfuːd ˌprəʊsesə(r); US ˈfuːd ˌprɒsesər/ **20**/25
**foot** /fʊt/ **3**/13
**football** /ˈfʊtbɔːl/ **78**/11, 12, **81**
**footbrake** /ˈfʊtbreɪk/ **64**/27
**footbridge** /ˈfʊtbrɪdʒ/ **62**/22
**forehead** /ˈfɒrɪd, also ˈfɔːhed; US ˈfɔːrɪd/ **4**/18
**foreign currency** /ˌfɒrən ˈkʌrənsɪ/ **34**/13
**forest** /ˈfɒrɪst; US ˈfɔːrɪst/ **73**/5
**fork** /fɔːk/ **15**/12, **22**/18
**fork-lift truck** /ˈfɔːklɪft trʌk/ **63**/8
**form** /fɔːm/ **43**/5
**Fort Worth** /ˌfɔːt ˈwɜːθ/ **55**
**forty** /ˈfɔːtɪ/ **33**/40
**four** /fɔː(r)/ **33**/4
**fourteen** /ˌfɔːˈtiːn/ **33**/14
**fourth** /fɔːθ/ **33**
**fox** /fɒks/ **89**/7
**fraction** /ˈfrækʃn/ **48**/18
**frame** /freɪm/ **8**/18, **15**/24, **65**/4
**France** /frɑːns; US fræns/ **54**
**freesia** /ˈfriːzɪə; US ˈfriːʒər/ **25**/20
**freeway** /ˈfriːweɪ/ **62**/11
**freezer** /ˈfriːzə(r)/ **20**/15
**freezing** /ˈfriːzɪŋ/ **52**/7
**French fries** /ˈfrentʃ fraɪz/ **28**/27
**French Guiana** /ˌfrentʃ gɪˈɑːnə, gɪˈænə/ **53**
**French horn** /ˌfrentʃ ˈhɔːn/ **75**/6
**Friday** /ˈfraɪdɪ/ **33**
**fridge** /frɪdʒ/ **20**/14
**friend** /frend/ **42**/20
**fringe** /frɪndʒ/ **5**/14
**frog** /frɒg/ **92**/25
**from** /frɒm/ **57**/7
**front** /frʌnt/ **48**/7
**front desk** /ˌfrʌnt ˈdesk/ **71**/1
**front door** /ˌfrʌnt ˈdɔː(r)/ **14**/3
**front garden** /ˌfrʌnt ˈgɑːdn/ **22**/21
**front teeth** /ˌfrʌnt tiːθ/ **8**/11
**front walk** /ˌfrʌnt wɔːk/ **22**/23
**front yard** /ˌfrʌnt ˈjɑːrd/ **22**/21
**frown (verb)** /fraʊn/ **84**/19
**fruit** /fruːt/ **24**, **28**/7
**fruit cocktail** /ˌfruːt ˈkɒkteɪl/ **28**/11
**frying-pan** /ˈfraɪɪŋ pæn/ **20**/24
**fuel gauge** /ˈfjuːəl geɪdʒ/ **64**/23
**fuel truck** /ˈfjuːəl trʌk/ **63**/3
**full** /fʊl/ **50**/3, **88**/11
**full slip** /fʊl slɪp/ **11**/5
**funnel** /ˈfʌnl/ **45**/10, **70**/10
**fur** /fɜː(r)/ **89**/20
**furrow** /ˈfʌrəʊ/ **73**/30
**fuselage** /ˈfjuːzəlɑːʒ/ **68**/17

**Gabon** /ˈgæbɒn/ **54**

**Galapagos Islands** /gəˈlæpəgɒs ˌaɪləndz/ **53**
**galaxy** /ˈgæləksɪ/ **50**/24
**gall-bladder** /ˈgɔːl blædə(r)/ **4**/5
**gallery** /ˈgælərɪ/ **76**/22
**Galway** /ˈgɔːlweɪ/ **56**
**Gambia** /ˈgæmbɪə/ **54**
**garage** /ˈgærɑːʒ, ˈgærɪdʒ; US gəˈrɑːʒ/ **14**/2
**garbage can** /ˈgɑːbɪdʒ ˌkæn/ **22**/20, **59**/14
**garden** /ˈgɑːdn/ **22**
**gardener** /ˈgɑːdnə(r)/ **39**/2
**garlic** /ˈgɑːlɪk/ **23**/2
**gas gauge** /ˈgæs geɪdʒ/ **64**/23
**gas pedal** /ˈgæs pedl/ **64**/28
**gas pump** /ˈgæs pʌmp/ **64**/11
**gas station** /ˈgæs steɪʃn/ **64**/1
**gate** /geɪt/ **22**/22, **66**/22, **67**/15
**gateau** /ˈgætəʊ; US gæˈtəʊ/ **28**/13
**gauze** /gɔːz/ **45**/25
**gauze pad** /ˈgɔːz pæd/ **7**/9
**gear changer** /ˈgɪər tʃeɪndʒər/ **65**/13
**gear lever** /ˈgɪə liːvə(r)/ **64**/21, **65**/13
**gearshift** /ˈgɪərʃɪft/ **64**/21
**Georgia** /ˈdʒɔːdʒə/ **54**
**Georgia** /ˈdʒɔːrdʒə/ **55**
**Germany** /ˈdʒɜːmənɪ/ **54**
**get dressed (verb)** /get ˈdrest/ **41**/8
**get out (verb)** /get ˈaʊt/ **41**/2
**get up (verb)** /get ˈʌp/ **41**/2
**Ghana** /ˈgɑːnə/ **54**
**gill** /gɪl/ **91**/4
**ginger** /ˈdʒɪndʒə(r)/ **5**/12
**giraffe** /dʒɪˈrɑːf; US dʒəˈræf/ **90**/23
**girl** /gɜːl/ **5**/3
**give (verb)** /gɪv/ **85**/9
**give way** /gɪv ˈweɪ/ **61**/1
**Glasgow** /ˈglɑːzgəʊ, ˈglæzgəʊ/ **56**
**glass** /glɑːs; US glæs/ **13**/23, **15**/14
**glass rod** /ˌglɑːs ˈrɒd; US ˌglæs-/ **46**/2
**glasses** /ˈglɑːsɪz; US ˈglæsɪz/ **8**/15
**glasses case** /ˈglɑːsɪz ˌkeɪs; US ˈglæsɪz/ **8**/19
**globe** /gləʊb/ **49**/11
**Gloucester** /ˈglɒstə(r)/ **56**
**Gloucestershire** /ˈglɒstəʃə(r)/ **56**
**glove** /glʌv/ **10**/15
**glue** /gluː/ **49**/23
**go (verb)** /gəʊ/ **41**/3, 4, **42**/24, **57**/6
**goal** /gəʊl/ **81**/23, 28
**goal-post** /ˈgəʊlpəʊst/ **81**/27
**goalkeeper** /ˈgəʊlkiːpə(r)/ **81**/30
**goat** /gəʊt/ **89**/8
**goggles** /ˈgɒglz/ **45**/1
**golf** /gɒlf/ **79**/11
**good** /gʊd/ **88**/5
**goose** /guːs/ **93**/27
**gorilla** /gəˈrɪlə/ **90**/14
**grade crossing** /greɪd ˈkrɒsɪŋ/ **66**/2
**graduated beaker** /ˌgrædʒʊeɪtɪd ˈbiːkər/ **45**/24
**graduated cylinder** /ˌgrædʒʊeɪtɪd ˈsɪlɪndər/ **46**/3
**grain** /greɪn/ **73**/27
**gram** /græm/ **48**/24
**granddaughter** /ˈgrænˌdɔːtə(r)/ **1**/23
**grandfather** /ˈgrændˌfɑːðə(r)/ **1**/2
**grandmother** /ˈgrændˌmʌðə(r)/ **1**/1
**grandparent** /ˈgrændˌpeərənt/ **1**/21
**grandson** /ˈgrændsʌn/ **1**/22
**grape** /greɪp/ **24**/10
**grapefruit** /ˈgreɪpfruːt/ **24**/21

**graphic equalizer** /ˌgræfɪk ˈiːkwəlaɪzə(r)/ **30**/17
**grass** /grɑːs; US græs/ **22**/3
**grass verge** /grɑːs ˈvɜːdʒ/ **62**/23
**grasshopper** /ˈgrɑːshɒpə(r); US ˈgræshɒpər/ **92**/17
**gray** /greɪ/ **9**/15
**Great Britain** /ˌgreɪt ˈbrɪtn/ **56**
**Great Falls** /ˌgreɪt ˈfɔːlz/ **55**
**Greater London** /ˌgreɪtə ˈlʌndən/ **56**
**Greater Manchester** /ˌ- ˈmæntʃəstə(r)/ **56**
**Greece** /griːs/ **54**
**green** /griːn/ **9**/11, 12, **79**/14
**green pepper** /ˌgriːn ˈpepə(r)/ **23**/3
**Greenland** /ˈgriːnlənd/ **53**
**greetings card** /ˈgriːtɪŋz kɑːd/ **32**/4
**grey** /greɪ/ **9**/15
**ground** /graʊnd/ **57**/5
**ground floor** /ˌgraʊnd ˈflɔː(r)/ **13**/14
**groundsheet** /ˈgraʊnd ʃiːt/ **71**/20
**grow (verb)** /grəʊ/ **57**/3, 12
**guarantee** /ˈgærən tiː/ **34**/3
**guardrail** /ˈgɑːrdˌreɪl/ **62**/19
**Guatemala** /ˌgwɑːtəˈmɑːlə/ **53**
**guest** /gest/ **71**/3
**Guinea** /ˈgɪnɪ/ **54**
**Guinea-Bissau** /ˌgɪnɪ bɪˈsəʊ/ **54**
**gulf** /gʌlf/ **53**
**Gulf of Alaska** /ˌgʌlf əv əˈlæskə/ **53**/16
**Gulf of Guinea** /ˌgʌlf əv ˈgɪnɪ/ **54**/24
**Gulf of Mexico** /ˌgʌlf əv ˈmeksɪkəʊ/ **53**/18
**gum** /gʌm/ **8**/7
**gutter** /ˈgʌtə(r)/ **14**/22, **59**/8
**Guyana** /gaɪˈænə/ **53**
**gym** /dʒɪm/ **82**/15
**gymnasium** /dʒɪmˈneɪzɪəm/ **82**/15
**gymnast** /ˈdʒɪmnæst/ **80**/2
**gymnastics** /dʒɪmˈnæstɪks/ **80**/1
**gypsy** /ˈdʒɪpsɪ/ **12**/5

**hair** /heə(r)/ **3**/2, 5, **84**/13–16
**hair-drier (or -dryer)** /ˈheədraɪə(r)/ **18**/20
**hairbrush** /ˈheəbrʌʃ/ **18**/8
**hairdresser** /ˈheədresə(r)/ **39**/5
**Haiti** /ˈheɪtɪ/ **53**
**half** /hɑːf; US hæf/ **27**/14, **37**/9, **48**/21, **50**/2, 4
**half moon** /hɑːf ˈmuːn; US hæf/ **50**/2, 4
**half slip** /ˈhɑːf slɪp; US ˈhæf slɪp/ **11**/8
**hammer** /ˈhæmə(r)/ **21**/16
**hamper** /ˈhæmpər/ **17**/16
**Hampshire** /ˈhæmpʃə(r)/ **56**
**hamster** /ˈhæmstə(r)/ **89**/25
**hand** /hænd/ **3**/19, **85**/1
**hand drill** /ˈhænd drɪl/ **21**/18
**hand-towel** /ˈhændtaʊəl/ **17**/10
**handbag** /ˈhændbæg/ **10**/10
**handkerchief** /ˈhæŋkətʃɪf, also -tʃiːf/ **10**/21
**handle** /ˈhændl/ **30**/9
**handlebar** /ˈhændlbɑː(r)/ **65**/19
**handsaw** /ˈhændsɔː/ **21**/22
**hang-glider** /ˈhæŋˌglaɪdə(r)/ **72**/23
**hang-gliding** /ˈhæŋˌglaɪdɪŋ/ **72**/22
**hanger** /ˈhæŋər/ **18**/18
**happy** /ˈhæpɪ/ **88**/1
**hard** /hɑːd/ **88**/17
**hard shoulder** /ˌhɑːd ˈʃəʊldə(r)/ **62**/4
**harmonica** /hɑːˈmɒnɪkə/ **75**/25
**harness** /ˈhɑːnɪs/ **72**/26
**Hartlepool** /ˈhɑːtlɪpuːl/ **56**

hat /hæt/ **12**/17
hatchback /ˈhætʃbæk/ **63**/15
hatchet /ˈhætʃɪt/ **21**/17
have (verb) /hæv/ **6**/4–14, **41**/7, 9, **42**/16
Hawaii /həˈwɑɪi:/ **55**
Hawaiian Islands /həˈwaɪən ˌaɪləndz/ **53**
hawk /hɔ:k/ **93**/10
head /hed/ **3**/1, **5**/7
headache /ˈhedeɪk/ **6**/6
headboard /ˈhedbɔ:d/ **18**/13
headlight /ˈhedlaɪt/ **64**/4
headphones /ˈhedfəʊnz/ **30**/12
health care /ˈhelθ keə(r)/ **7**/8
health club /ˈhelθ klʌb/ **42**/19
heart /hɑ:t/ **4**/4, **74**/32
heavy /ˈhevi/ **88**/14
hedge /hedʒ/ **22**/27
hedgehog /ˈhedʒhɒg/ **89**/5
heel /hi:l/ **3**/15, **11**/20
height /haɪt/ **48**/2
helicopter /ˈhelɪkɒptə(r)/ **68**/9
helmet /ˈhelmɪt/ **12**/2
hen /hen/ **93**/2
Hereford and Worcester /ˌherɪfəd ənd
  ˈwʊstə(r)/ **56**
herring /ˈherɪŋ/ **91**/6
Hertfordshire /ˈhɑ:tfədʃə(r)/ **56**
hi-fi /haɪfaɪ/ **30**/13
hi-fi shop /ˈhaɪfaɪ ʃɒp/ **30**
high /haɪ/ **87**/17
Highland /ˈhaɪlənd/ **56**
highway /ˈhaɪweɪ/ **62**/24
hiker /ˈhaɪkə(r)/ **71**/24
hiking /ˈhaɪkɪŋ/ **71**/23
hill /hɪl/ **73**/12
hip-bone /ˈhɪpbəʊn/ **4**/15
hippopotamus /ˌhɪpəˈpɒtəməs/ **90**/22
hit (verb) /hɪt/ **78**/28
hobby /ˈhɒbi/ **74**
hockey /ˈhɒki/ **78**/16
hockey ball /ˈhɒki bɔ:l/ **78**/19
hockey player /ˈhɒki pleɪə(r)/ **78**/17
hockey stick /ˈhɒki stɪk/ **78**/18
hold (verb) /həʊld/ **86**/15
hole /həʊl/ **79**/16
hole-punch /ˈhəʊlpʌntʃ/ **44**/7
holiday /ˈhɒlideɪ/ **71**/72
holiday resort /ˈhɒlideɪ rɪˌzɔ:t/ **72**/2
hollow /ˈhɒləʊ/ **88**/21
Hollywood /ˈhɒliwʊd/ **55**
home /həʊm/ **41**/10
Honduras /hɒnˈdjʊərəs; US - dʊərəs/ **53**
Honolulu /ˌhɒnəˈlu:lu:/ **55**
hood /hʊd/ **64**/14
hoof /hu:f/ **89**/12
hook /hʊk/ **19**/16
Hoover /ˈhu:və(r)/ **19**/7
horn /hɔ:n/ **90**/20
horse /hɔ:s/ **89**/13
horse-racing /ˈhɔ:sreɪsɪŋ/ **80**/23
horseback riding /ˈhɔ:rsbæk ˌraɪdɪŋ/ **72**/16,
  **80**/9
hose /həʊz/ **38**/12, **64**/12, **83**/8
hospital room /ˈhɒspɪtl ru:m, rʊm/ **7**
hospital ward /ˈhɒspɪtl wɔ:d/ **7**
hot /hɒt/ **52**/3
hot water faucet /ˈhɒt wɔ:tər ˌfɔ:sɪt/ **19**/20
hot-air balloon /ˌhɒtˈeə bəˌlu:n/ **72**/21
hot(-water) tap /ˌhɒtˈwɔ:tə ˌtæp/ **19**/20

hotel reception /həʊˌtel rɪˈsepʃn/ **71**/1
hour /ˈaʊə(r)/ **37**
hour-hand /ˈaʊəhænd/ **37**/4
Houston /ˈhju:stən/ **55**
hovercraft /ˈhɒvəkrɑ:ft; US -kræft/ **70**/8
hub /hʌb/ **65**/12
Hudson /ˈhʌdsn/ **55**
Hudson Bay /ˌhʌdsn ˈbeɪ/ **53**/17
hug (verb) /hʌg/ **85**/3
human body /ˌhju:mən ˈbɒdi/ **3**/4
hummingbird /ˈhʌmɪŋbɜ:d/ **93**/16
hump /hʌmp/ **90**/11
hundred /ˈhʌndrəd/ **33**/100
Hungary /ˈhʌŋgəri/ *US* ˈhʌŋgri/ **54**
hungry /ˈhʌŋgri/ **6**/2
hurt (verb) /hɜ:t/ **6**/12
husband /ˈhʌzbənd/ **1**/18
hydrant /ˈhaɪdrənt/ **38**/11
hydrofoil /ˈhaɪdrəfɔɪl/ **70**/7
hypotenuse /haɪˈpɒtənju:z; *US* haɪˈpɒtnu:s/
  **47**/17

ice-cream /ˌaɪsˈkri:m, *esp US* ˈaɪskri:m/ **28**/10
ice-rink /ˈaɪsrɪŋk/ **77**/5
ice-skating /ˈaɪsskeɪtɪŋ/ **77**/1
Iceland /ˈaɪslənd/ **54**
Idaho /ˈaɪdəhəʊ/ **55**
Idaho Falls /ˌaɪdəhəʊ ˈfɔ:lz/ **55**
ignition /ɪgˈnɪʃn/ **64**/25
Illinois /ˌɪləˈnɔɪ/ **55**
in /ɪn/ **58**/3, 7
in box /ˈɪn bɒks/ **44**/3
in front of /ɪn ˈfrʌnt əv/ **58**/18
in the middle of /ɪn ðə ˈmɪdl əv/ **58**/13
in-tray /ˈɪntreɪ/ **44**/3
India /ˈɪndɪə/ **54**
Indian /ˈɪndɪən/ **53**/12
Indiana /ˌɪndɪˈænə/ **55**
Indianapolis /ˌɪndɪəˈnæpəlɪs/ **55**
indicator /ˈɪndɪkeɪtə(r)/ **64**/3
Indonesia /ˌɪndəˈni:zɪə; *US* ˌɪndəˈni:ʒə/ **54**
inflatable dinghy /ɪnˌfleɪtəbl ˈdɪŋgi/ **70**/14
injection /ɪnˈdʒekʃn/ **7**/21
injured /ˈɪndʒəd/ **38**/15
insect /ˈɪnsekt/ **92**
inside /ˈɪnsaɪd/ **58**/3
inside lane /ˈɪnsaɪd leɪn/ **62**/5
instructor /ɪnˈstrʌktə(r)/ **82**/7
internal /ɪnˈtɜ:nl/ **4**/1
international code /ˌɪntəˈnæʃnəl kəʊd/ **38**/18
intersection /ˌɪntəˈsekʃn/ **60**/21, **62**/25
interstate highway /ˌɪntəsteɪt ˈhaɪweɪ/ **62**/11
intestines /ɪnˈtestɪnz/ **4**/9
into /ˈɪntu:/ **57**/4
Inverclyde /ˌɪnvəˈklaɪd/ **56**
Inverness /ˌɪnvəˈnes/ **56**
Iowa /ˈaɪəwə/ **55**
Ipswich /ˈɪpswɪtʃ/ **56**
Iran /ɪˈrɑ:n/ **54**
Iraq /ɪˈrɑ:k/ **54**
iris /ˈaɪərɪs/ **4**/29, **25**/28
Irish Sea /ˌaɪrɪʃ ˈsi:/ **56**
iron (verb) /ˈaɪən; *US* aɪərn/ **83**/1
iron /ˈaɪən; *US* ˈaɪərn/ **19**/13
ironing-board /ˈaɪənɪŋ bɔ:d; *US* ˈaɪərnɪŋ
  bɔ:rd/ **19**/9
island /ˈaɪlənd/ **55**
Isle of Man /ˌaɪl əv ˈmæn/ **56**

Isle of Wight /ˌaɪl əv ˈwaɪt/ **56**
Isles of Scilly /ˌaɪlz əv ˈsɪli/ **56**
Israel /ˈɪzreɪl/ **54**
Italy /ˈɪtəli/ **54**

jack /dʒæk/ **74**/31
jacket /ˈdʒækɪt/ **10**/8
jacket potato /ˌdʒækɪt pəˈteɪtəʊ/ **28**/25
jackhammer /ˈdʒækhæmər/ **61**/16
Jackson /ˈdʒæksən/ **55**
Jacksonville /ˈdʒæksənvɪl/ **55**
jam /dʒæm/ **27**/5, 17
Jamaica /dʒəˈmeɪkə/ **53**
January /ˈdʒænjʊəri; *US* ˈdʒænjʊeri/ **52**
Japan /dʒəˈpæn/ **54**
jar /dʒɑ:(r)/ **27**/5
jaw /dʒɔ:/ **3**/4
JCB /ˌdʒeɪ si: ˈbi:/ **61**/18
jeans /dʒi:nz/ **10**/7
jeep /dʒi:p/ **63**/10
jellyfish /ˈdʒelɪfɪʃ/ **91**/15
jet engine /ˌdʒet ˈendʒɪn/ **68**/19
jewellery (*esp US* jewelry) /ˈdʒu:əlri/ **12**
job /dʒɒb/ **39**/40
jockey /ˈdʒɒki/ **80**/26
jog (verb) /dʒɒg/ **82**/2
jogger /ˈdʒɒgə(r)/ **82**/3
jogging suit /ˈdʒɒgɪŋ ˌsu:t/ **12**/3
joint /dʒɔɪnt/ **27**/7
Jordan /ˈdʒɔ:dn/ **54**
judo /ˈdʒu:dəʊ/ **79**/26
jug /dʒʌg/ **15**/17
July /dʒu:ˈlaɪ/ **52**
jump (verb) /dʒʌmp/ **78**/21
jump rope /ˈdʒʌmp rəʊp/ **82**/26
junction /ˈdʒʌŋkʃn/ **62**/25
June /dʒu:n/ **52**
Jupiter /ˈdʒu:pɪtə(r)/ **50**/19

Kampuchea /ˌkæmpʊˈtʃɪə/ **54**
kangaroo /ˌkæŋgəˈru:/ **90**/8
Kansas /ˈkænzəs/ **55**
Kansas City /ˌkænzəs ˈsɪti/ **55**
Kara Sea /ˌkɑːrəˈsi:; *US* ˈkærə/ **54**/40
karate /kəˈrɑ:ti/ **79**/27
kayak /ˈkaɪæk/ **69**/19
Kazakhstan /ˌkæzækˈstɑ:n/ **54**
keeping fit /ˌki:pɪŋ ˈfɪt/ **82**
keeping in shape /ˌki:pɪŋ ɪn ˈʃeɪp/ **82**
Kent /kent/ **56**
Kentucky /kenˈtʌki/ **55**
Kenya /ˈkenjə/ **54**
kerb /kɜ:b/ **59**/9
Kerry /ˈkeri/ **56**
kettle /ˈketl/ **20**/19, **83**/9
kettledrum /ˈketldrʌm/ **75**/17
key /ki:/ **44**/11, **56**, **75**/24
keyboard /ˈki:bɔ:d/ **44**/22
keyboard player /ˈki:bɔ:d ˌpleɪə(r)/ **76**/12
kidney /ˈkɪdni/ **4**/7
Kildare /kɪlˈdeə(r)/ **56**
Kilkenny /kɪlˈkeni/ **56**
kilogram /ˈkɪləgræm/ **48**/25
kilometre /ˈkɪləmi:tə(r), kɪˈlɒmɪtə(r)/ **48**
king /kɪŋ/ **74**/33
Kingston upon Hull /ˌkɪŋstən əpɒn ˈhʌl/ **56**
Kirgyzstan /ˌkɪəgɪˈstɑ:n/ **54**

kiss (verb) /kɪs/ 85/2
kit /kɪt/ 74/7
kitchen /'kɪtʃɪn/ 20
kitten /'kɪtn/ 89/21
kiwi fruit /'kiːwiː fruːt/ 24/18
knave /neɪv/ 74/31
knee /niː/ 3/18
kneecap /'niːkæp/ 4/16
kneel (verb) /niːl/ 82/21
knife /naɪf/ 15/10
knitting /'nɪtɪŋ/ 74/21
knitting-needle /'nɪtɪŋ niːdl/ 74/23
knocker /'nɒkə(r)/ 13/4
Kuwait /kʊ'weɪt/ 54

lab coat /'læb kəʊt/ 46/1
label /'leɪbl/ 32/3
ladder /'lædə(r)/ 38/5
ladle /'leɪdl/ 20/11
ladybird /'leɪdibɜːd/ 92/14
ladybug /'leɪdibʌg/ 92/14
lake /leɪk/ 55/3
Lake Erie /ˌleɪk 'ɪəri/ 55
Lake Huron /ˌleɪk 'hjʊərɒn/ 55
Lake Michigan /ˌleɪk 'mɪʃɪgən/ 55
Lake Ontario /ˌleɪk ɒn'teəriəʊ/ 55
Lake Superior /ˌleɪk suː'pɪəriər/ 55
lamb /læm/ 89/10
lamb chop /ˌlæm 'tʃɒp/ US 'læm tʃɒp/ 28/19
lamp /læmp/ 15/22
lamppost /'læmppəʊst/ 60/7
lampshade /'læmpʃeɪd/ 15/23
Lanarkshire /'lænəkʃə(r)/ 56
Lancashire /'læŋkəʃə(r)/ 56
landing /'lændɪŋ/ 68/8
lane /leɪn/ 80/19
Laois /liːʃ/ 56
Laos /laːɒs/ 54
Laptev Sea /ˌlæptev 'siː/ 54/39
Laramie /'lærəmi/ 55
large /lɑːdʒ/ 87/3
Larne /lɑːn/ 56
Las Vegas /lɒs 'veɪgəs/ 55
last quarter /ˌlɑːst 'kwɔːrtər/ 50/4
Latvia /'lætviə/ 54
laugh (verb) /lɑːf/ US læf/ 84/18
launch pad /'lɔːntʃ pæd/ 50/12
laundry basket /'lɔːndri bɑːskɪt/ 17/16
laundry room /'lɔːndri ruːm, rʊm/ 19
lawn /lɔːn/ 22/3
lawnmower /'lɔːnməʊə(r)/ 22/5
leaf /liːf/ 25/11
leave (verb) /liːv/ 41/10
Lebanon /'lebənən/ US 'lebənɒn/ 54
Leeds /liːdz/ 56
left lane /ˌleft leɪn/ 62/17
leg /leg/ 3/12, 6/12, 13
Leicester /'lestə(r)/ 56
Leicestershire /'lestəʃə(r)/ 56
Leitrim /'liːtrɪm/ 56
lemon /'lemən/ 24/6
length /leŋθ/ 48/6
lens /lenz/ 8/16, 29/17
leopard /'lepəd/ 90/18
Lesotho /le'suːtuː/ 54
letter /'letə(r)/ 32/5, 43/1, 3, 4, 6, 10
letter-box /'letəbɒks/ 13/5, 31/11, 14, 59/3
lettuce /'letɪs/ 23/7
level /'levəl/ 21/7

level crossing /ˌlevl 'krɒsɪŋ/ 66/2
Liberia /laɪ'bɪriə/ 54
library /'laɪbrəri/ US 'laɪbreri/ 57/6, 7
Libya /'lɪbiə/ 54
license plate /'laɪsns pleɪt/ 64/5
lid /lɪd/ 15/5
lie down (verb) /ˌlaɪ 'daʊn/ 84/23
lifeboat /'laɪfbəʊt/ 69/18
lift (verb) /lɪft/ 86/13
light (verb) /laɪt/ 86/23
light /laɪt/ 9/11, 18/16, 88/13
light switch /'laɪt swɪtʃ/ 18/27
light-bulb /'laɪtbʌlb/ 19/15
lighthouse /'laɪthaʊs/ 70/12
lightning /'laɪtnɪŋ/ 51/11
lily /'lɪli/ 25/26
Limavady /ˌlɪmə'vædi/ 56
lime /laɪm/ 24/17
Limerick /'lɪmərɪk/ 56
Lincoln /'lɪŋkən/ 55
Lincolnshire /'lɪŋkənʃə(r)/ 56
line /laɪn/ 47/25, 26, 29, 30, 66/7, 12, 69/6
liner /'laɪnə(r)/ 70/11
linesman /'laɪnzmən/ 81/25
lion /'laɪən/ 90/16
lip /lɪp/ 4/23
lipstick /'lɪpstɪk/ 12/21
Lisburn /'lɪzbən/ 56
listen (verb) /'lɪsn/ 41/12
Lithuania /ˌlɪθju'eɪniə/ 54
litre /'liːtə(r)/ 48/28
litter-bin /'lɪtəbɪn/ 59/14
little /'lɪtl/ 87/4
Little Rock /ˌlɪtl rɒk/ 55
liver /'lɪvə(r)/ 4/6
Liverpool /'lɪvəpuːl/ 56
living-room /'lɪvɪŋ ruːm, rʊm/ 16
lizard /'lɪzəd/ 91/28
llama /'lɑːmə/ 90/12
loaf /ləʊf/ 27/2
lobster /'lɒbstə(r)/ 91/16
lock /lɒk/ 18/26, 65/6
log /lɒg/ 16/5
London /'lʌndən/ 56
Londonderry /ˌlʌndən'deri/ 56
long /lɒŋ/ 5/12, 15
Longford /'lɒŋfəd/ 56
look (verb) /lʊk/ 57/1, 14
loose /luːs/ 88/24
lorry /'lɒri/ 63/4
lorry driver /'lɒri draɪvə(r)/ 40/2
Los Angeles /lɒs 'ændʒəliz/ 55
Lothian /'ləʊðiən/ 56
lotion /'ləʊʃn/ 17/21
loud /laʊd/ 88/3
Louisiana /luːˌiːzi'ænə/ 55
Louisville /'luːɪvɪl/ 55
Louth /laʊθ/ 56
low /ləʊ/ 87/18
luggage /'lʌgɪdʒ/ 67/17
luggage reclaim /'lʌgɪdʒ rɪˌkleɪm/ 67/16
lunar module /ˌluːnə 'mɒdjuːl; US 'mɒdʒuːl/ 50/5
lunar vehicle /ˌluːnə 'viːəkl; US 'viːhɪkl/ 50/8
lunch /lʌntʃ/ 42/17
lung /lʌŋ/ 4/3
lychee (also litchi) /ˌlaɪ'tʃiː, 'laɪtʃiː; US 'liːtʃiː/ 24/15

Macedonia /ˌmæsɪ'dəʊnjə/ 54
Madagascar /ˌmædə'gæskə(r)/ 54
magazine /mægə'ziːn; US 'mægəziːn/ 26/7
Magherafelt /'mækərəfelt/ 56
magnet /'mægnɪt/ 46/8
magnifying glass /'mægnɪfaɪɪŋ glɑːs; US -glæs/ 45/14
mail /meɪl/ 31/10, 41/6
mail truck /'meɪl trʌk/ 31/7
mailbag /'meɪlbæg/ 31/9, 13
mailbox /'meɪlbɒks/ 13/5, 31/11, 14, 59/3
mailman /'meɪlmæn/ 31/8
main course /'meɪn kɔːs/ 28
main river /meɪn rɪvə(r)/ 55
Maine /meɪn/ 55
make (verb) /meɪk/ 74/6
make a deposit (verb) /ˌmeɪk ə dɪ'pɒzɪt/ 34/17
make a note (verb) /ˌmeɪk ə 'nəʊt/ 43/8
make-up /'meɪkʌp/ 12/20
Malawi /mə'lɑːwi/ 54
Malaysia /mə'leɪziə; US mə'leɪʒə/ 54
Mali /'mɑːli/ 54
mallet /'mælɪt/ 21/2
man /mæn/ 5/5, 6, 38/15
Manchester /'mæntʃɪstə(r)/ 56
mane /meɪn/ 89/16
mango /'mæŋgəʊ/ 24/19
manhole cover /'mænhəʊl kʌvə(r)/ 59/7
mantel /'mæntl/ 16/2, 58/9, 10
mantelpiece /'mæntlpiːs/ 16/2, 58/9, 10
map /mæp/ 49/18
March /mɑːtʃ/ 52
margarine /ˌmɑːdʒə'riːn; US 'mɑːrdʒərɪn/ 27/20, 28
marina /mə'riːnə/ 69/10
market /'mɑːkɪt/ 23/24, 23/1
Mars /mɑːz/ 50/20
Maryland /'meərilənd/ 55
mask /mɑːsk; US mæsk/ 7/17
Massachusetts /ˌmæsə'tʃuːsɪts/ 55
mast /mɑːst; US mæst/ 69/2
mat /mæt/ 82/17
match /mætʃ/ 81/1, 8, 12
matter /'mætə(r)/ 6
mattress /'mætrɪs/ 18/11
Mauritania /ˌmɒrɪ'teɪniə; US ˌmɔːr-/ 54
Mauritius /mə'rɪʃəs; US mɔː'rɪʃəs/ 54
May /meɪ/ 52
Mayo /'meɪəʊ/ 56
meal /miːl/ 83/2
measurement /'meʒəmənt/ 48
measuring beaker /'meʒərɪŋ biːkə(r)/ 45/24
measuring cylinder /'meʒərɪŋ sɪlɪndə(r)/ 46/3
meat /miːt/ 27/8
Meath /miːθ/ 56
mechanic /mɪ'kænɪk/ 40/11
median strip /'miːdiən strɪp/ 62/18
medicine /'medsn; US 'medɪsn/ 7/1
medicine chest /'medsn tʃest/ 17/1
Mediterranean Sea /ˌmedɪtə,reɪniən 'siː/ 54/23
meet (verb) /miːt/ 42/20
melon /'melən/ 24/1, 28/2
Memphis /'memfɪs/ 55
menu /'menjuː/ 28/15
Mercury /'mɜːkjʊri/ 50/23
Merseyside /'mɜːzɪsaɪd/ 56

Merthyr Tydfil /ˌmɜːθə ˈtɪdvɪl/ 56
message /ˈmesɪdʒ/ 32/9
messenger /ˈmesɪndʒər/ 31/15, 16
messy /ˈmesɪ/ 88/8
metal detector /ˈmetl dɪˌtektə(r)/ 67/8
Mexico /ˈmeksɪkəʊ/ 53
mezzanine /ˈmezəniːn/ 76/21
Miami /maɪˈæmɪ/ 55
Michigan /ˈmɪʃɪɡən/ 55
microbalance /ˈmaɪkrəʊbæləns/ 46/27
microphone /ˈmaɪkrəfəʊn/ 30/2
microscope /ˈmaɪkrəskəʊp/ 46/17
midday /ˈmɪdˈdeɪ/ 37/13
middle lane /ˌmɪdl leɪn/ 62/6, 16
Middlesbrough /ˈmɪdlzbərə/ 56
Midlothian /mɪdˈləʊðɪən/ 56
midnight /ˈmɪdnaɪt/ 37/13
milk /mɪlk/ 27/24
millilitre /ˈmɪlɪliːtə(r)/ 48/27
millimetre /ˈmɪlɪmiːtə(r)/ 48/29
million /ˈmɪljən/ 33/1000000
Milwaukee /mɪlˈwɔːkɪ/ 55
mineral water /ˈmɪnərəl wɔːtə(r)/ 27/25
Minneapolis /ˌmɪnɪˈæpəlɪs/ 55
Minnesota /ˌmɪnəˈsəʊtə/ 55
minus /ˈmaɪnəs/ 48/12, 52/8
minute /ˈmɪnɪt/ 37/14
minute-hand /ˈmɪnɪt hænd/ 37/3
mirror /ˈmɪrə(r)/ 15/1
miss (verb) /mɪs/ 81/29
Mississippi /ˌmɪsɪˈsɪpɪ/ 55
Missouri /mɪˈzʊərɪ/ 55
misty /ˈmɪstɪ/ 51/6
mitt /mɪt/ 78/4
mixer /ˈmɪksə(r)/ 20/8
mixing bowl /ˈmɪksɪŋ bəʊl/ 20/3
Mobile /ˈməʊbiːl/ 55
model /ˈmɒdl/ 74/6, 8
Moldova /mɒlˈdəʊvə/ 54
Monaghan /ˈmɒnəhən/ 56
Monday /ˈmʌndɪ/ 33
money /ˈmʌnɪ/ 34/12, 35/36
money order /ˈmʌnɪ ɔːrdər/ 32/23
Mongolia /mɒŋˈɡəʊlə/ 54
monkey /ˈmʌŋkɪ/ 90/13
Monmouthshire /ˈmɒnməθʃə(r)/ 56
monster /ˈmɒnstə(r)/ 12/13
Montana /mɒnˈtænə/ 55
month /mʌnθ/ 52
monthly statement /ˌmʌnθlɪ ˈsteɪtmənt/ 34/5
moon /muːn/ 50/1, 2, 3, 4
mooring /ˈmʊərɪŋ/ 69/15
mop /mɒp/ 19/8
Moray /ˈmʌrɪ/ 56
morning /ˈmɔːnɪŋ/ 37/15
Morocco /məˈrɒkəʊ/ 54
mortar /ˈmɔːtə(r)/ 45/8
mosquito /məsˈkiːtəʊ, Brit also mɒs-/ 92/4
moth /mɒθ/ 92/9
mother /ˈmʌðə(r)/ 1/5
mother-in-law /ˈmʌðər ɪn lɔː/ 1/8
motor bike /ˈməʊtə baɪk/ 65/25
motor boat /ˈməʊtə bəʊt/ 69/11
motor cycle /ˈməʊtə ˌsaɪkl/ 65/25
motor-racing /ˈməʊtəˌreɪsɪŋ/ 80/5
motorway /ˈməʊtəweɪ/ 62/1
mountain /ˈmaʊntɪn; US ˈmaʊntn/ 55, 73/1
moustache /məˈstɑːʃ; US ˈmʌstæʃ/ 4/21
mouth /maʊθ/ 3/29

movie star /ˈmuːvɪ stɑːr/ 76/24
movie theater /ˈmuːvɪ θɪətər/ 76
Moyle /mɔɪl/ 56
Mozambique /ˌməʊzæmˈbiːk/ 54
mudguard /ˈmʌdɡɑːd/ 65/22
mug /mʌɡ/ 20/16, 58/5
multiplied by /ˈmʌltɪplaɪd baɪ/ 48/13
mushroom /ˈmʌʃrʊm, ˈmʌʃruːm/ 28/21
music /ˈmjuːzɪk/ 41/12, 76
musical instrument /ˈmjuːzɪkl ˈɪnstrʊmənt/ 75
musician /mjuːˈzɪʃn/ 76/2
mussel /ˈmʌsl/ 91/23
Myanmar /ˌmɪənˈmɑː(r)/ 54

nail /neɪl/ 3/17, 21/23
nail-brush /ˈneɪlbrʌʃ/ 17/5
Namibia /nəˈmɪbɪə/ 54
napkin /ˈnæpkɪn/ 15/7
narrow /ˈnærəʊ/ 87/16
Nashville /ˈnæʃvɪl/ 55
navy /ˈneɪvɪ/ 9/9
near /nɪə(r)/ 58/6
neat /niːt/ 88/7
Neath and Port Talbot /niːθ ənd ˌpɔːt ˈtɔːlbət/ 56
Nebraska /nəˈbræskə/ 55
neck /nek/ 3/5
necklace /ˈneklɪs/ 12/26
needle /ˈniːdl/ 74/19
negative /ˈneɡətɪv/ 29/10
Nepal /nɪˈpɔːl; US nəˈpɑːl/ 54
nephew /ˈnevjuː; US ˈnefjuː/ 1/15
Neptune /ˈneptjuːn; US ˈneptuːn/ 50/16
nest /nest/ 93/13
net /net/ 78/9, 81/7
Netherlands /ˈneðələndz/ 54
Nevada /nəˈvɑːdə/ 55
new /njuː; US nuː/ 87/6
New Caledonia /nuː kæləˈdəʊnjə/ 54
New Haven /ˌnuː ˈheɪvn/ 55
New Jersey /ˌnuː ˈdʒɜːrzɪ/ 55
New Mexico /ˌnuː ˈmeksɪkəʊ/ 55
new moon /njuː ˈmuːn/ 50/1
New Orleans /ˌnuː ˈɔːrlɪnz/ 55
New York /ˌnuː ˈjɔːrk/ 55
New Zealand /ˌnjuː (US ˌnuː) ˈziːlənd/ 54
Newcastle /ˈnjuːkɑːsl/ 56
Newport /ˈnjuːpɔːt/ 56
Newry and Mourne /ˌnjʊərɪ ənd ˈmɔːn/ 56
news-stand /ˈnjuːzstænd/ 59/15
news-vendor /ˈnjuːzvendə(r)/ 59/17
newsagent /ˈnjuːzeɪdʒənt/ 26
newscaster /ˈnuːzkæstər/ 39/4
newspaper /ˈnjuːzpeɪpə(r); US ˈnuːzpeɪpər/ 26/8, 41/11, 42/14, 59/16
newsreader /ˈnjuːzriːdə(r)/ 39/4
newsstand /ˈnuːzstænd/ 26
Newtownabbey /ˌnjuːtnˈæbɪ/ 56
next to /nekst tʊ/ 58/17
Niagara Falls /naɪˌæɡrə ˈfɔːlz/ 55
Nicaragua /ˌnɪkəˈræɡjʊə; US ˌnɪkəˈrɑːɡwə/ 53
nickel /ˈnɪkl/ 35/3
niece /niːs/ 1/14
Niger /naɪdʒə(r)/ 54
Nigeria /naɪˈdʒɪərɪə/ 54
night /naɪt/ 37/18
night table /ˈnaɪt teɪbl/ 18/10
night-dress /ˈnaɪtdres/ 11/11
nightgown /ˈnaɪtɡaʊn/ 11/11

nine /naɪn/ 33/9
nineteen /ˌnaɪnˈtiːn/ 33/19
ninety /ˈnaɪntɪ/ 33/90
ninth /naɪnθ/ 33
no entry /ˌnəʊ ˈentrɪ/ 61/3
no left turn /ˌnəʊ ˌleft ˈtɜːn/ 61/7
no U-turn /ˌnəʊ ˌjuːˈtɜːn/ 61/5
noon /nuːn/ 37/13
Norfolk /ˈnɔːfək/ 56
north /nɔːθ/ 56
North Korea /ˌnɔːθ kəˈrɪə/ 54
North Sea /ˌnɔːθ ˈsiː/ 54/21
Northamptonshire /nɔːˈθæmptənʃə(r)/ 56
Northern Ireland /ˌnɔːðən ˈaɪələnd/ 56
Northumberland /nɔːˈθʌmbələnd/ 56
Norway /ˈnɔːweɪ/ 54
Norwegian Sea /nɔːˌwiːdʒən ˈsiː/ 54/20
Norwich /ˈnɒrɪtʃ/ 56
nose /nəʊz/ 4/20, 68/13
note /nəʊt/ 36/10
notebook /ˈnəʊtbʊk/ 44/13, 49/4
notice /ˈnəʊtɪs/ 57/9, 10
notice-board /ˈnəʊtɪsbɔːd/ 44/1
Nottingham /ˈnɒtɪŋəm/ 56
Nottinghamshire /ˈnɒtɪŋəmʃə(r)/ 56
November /nəʊˈvembə(r)/ 52
nozzle /ˈnɒzl/ 64/13
number /ˈnʌmbə(r)/ 33
number-plate /ˈnʌmbə pleɪt/ 64/5
nurse /nɜːs/ 7/12
nut /nʌt/ 21/25, 24/12

o'clock /əˈklɒk/ 37/1, 13, 15, 16, 17
oar /ɔː(r)/ 69/8
objective lens /əbˈdʒektɪv lenz/ 46/21
oboe /ˈəʊbəʊ/ 75/13
obtuse angle /ɒbˌtjuːs ˈæŋɡl; US ɒbˌtuːs -/ 47/18
ocean /ˈəʊʃn/ 53
ocean liner /ˈəʊʃn laɪnər/ 70/11
October /ɒkˈtəʊbə(r)/ 52
octopus /ˈɒktəpəs/ 91/12
off /ɒf/ 57/8
Offaly /ˈɒfəlɪ/ 56
office /ˈɒfɪs; US ˈɔːfɪs/ 43/44
Ohio /əʊˈhaɪəʊ/ 55
(oil-)tanker /ɔɪl ˈtæŋkə(r)/ 70/6
ointment /ˈɔɪntmənt/ 7/8
Oklahoma /ˌəʊkləˈhəʊmə/ 55
Oklahoma City /ˌəʊkləˌhəʊmə ˈsɪtɪ/ 55
old /əʊld/ 5/6, 50/4, 87/5
Omagh /ˈəʊmɑː/ 56
Omaha /ˈəʊməhɑː/ 55
Oman /əʊˈmɑːn/ 54
on /ɒn/ 58/9
on top of /ɒn ˈtɒp əv/ 58/11
one /wʌn/ 33/1
one-family house /ˈwʌnˌfæməlɪ ˌhaʊs/ 14/1
one-way street /ˌwʌnweɪ ˈstriːt/ 61/10
onion /ˈʌnɪən/ 23/11
onto /ˈɒntuː/ 57/5
open (verb) /ˈəʊpən/ 85/11
open /ˈəʊpən/ 87/9
operating room /ˈɒpəreɪtɪŋ ruːm, rʊm/ 7/16
operating theatre /ˈɒpəreɪtɪŋ θɪətə(r)/ 7/16
operation /ˌɒpəˈreɪʃn/ 7
optician /ɒpˈtɪʃn/ 8/13
orange /ˈɒrɪndʒ; US ˈɔːrɪndʒ/ 9/3, 24/9
orange juice /ˈɒrɪndʒ dʒuːs; US ˈɔː-/ 27/21

orbit /ˈɔːbɪt/ **50**/13
orchestra /ˈɔːkɪstrə/ **76**/1
orchestra pit /ˈɔːkɪstrə pɪt/ **76**/19
orchestra seats /ˈɔːrkɪstrə siːts/ **76**/20
orchid /ˈɔːkɪd/ **25**/18
Oregon /ˈɒrɪɡən/ **55**
organ /ˈɔːɡən/ **4**/1
Orkney Islands /ˈɔːkni aɪləndz/ **56**
Orlando /ɔːˈlændəʊ/ **55**
ornament /ˈɔːnəmənt/ **58**/12
ostrich /ˈɒstrɪtʃ/ **93**/22
out box /ˈaʊt bɒks/ **44**/4
out of /ˈaʊt əv/ **57**/1
out-tray /ˈaʊtreɪ/ **44**/4
outboard motor /ˌaʊtbɔːd ˈməʊtə(r)/ **70**/15
outer space /ˌaʊtə ˈspeɪs/ **50**
outlet /ˈaʊtlet/ **19**/21
outside /ˈaʊtsaɪd/ **58**/1
outside lane /ˈaʊtsaɪd leɪn/ **62**/7
oval /ˈəʊvl/ **47**/8
oven /ˈʌvn/ **20**/22
oven glove /ˈʌvn ɡlʌv/ **20**/21
over /ˈəʊvə(r)/ **57**/14, **58**/10
overpass /ˈəʊvəpæs/ **62**/20
owl /aʊl/ **93**/12
Oxford /ˈɒksfəd/ **56**
Oxfordshire /ˈɒksfədʃə(r)/ **56**
oyster /ˈɔɪstə(r)/ **91**/21

pack /pæk/ **26**/3, 14, **74**/30
package /ˈpækɪdʒ/ **27**/16, **32**/1
packet /ˈpækɪt/ **26**/3, 14, 15, 16, **27**/16
paddle /ˈpædl/ **69**/20, **78**/27
pads /pædz/ **81**/15
pail /peɪl/ **19**/6
paintbox /ˈpeɪntbɒks/ **49**/15
paintbrush /ˈpeɪntbrʌʃ/ **49**/14
painting /ˈpeɪntɪŋ/ **15**/25, **74**/1
pair of /ˈpeər əv/ **8**/15, **49**/19
Pakistan /ˌpɑːkɪˈstɑːn; US ˈpækɪstæn/ **54**
palm /pɑːm/ **3**/22, **25**/16
Panama /ˈpænəmɑː/ **53**
panda /ˈpændə/ **90**/7
pants /pænts/ **10**/4, **11**/10
pantyhose /ˈpæntɪhəʊz/ **11**/7
papaya /pəˈpaɪə/ **24**/14
paper /ˈpeɪpə(r)/ **57**/4, 5, 8, **86**/17-19
paper bag /ˌpeɪpə ˈbæɡ/ **23**/22
paper-clip /ˈpeɪpəklɪp/ **44**/10
Papua New Guinea /ˌpæpʊəˌnju: (US ˌnuː) ˈɡɪni/ **54**
parachute /ˈpærəʃuːt/ **72**/19
parachuting /ˈpærəʃuːtɪŋ/ **72**/18
Paraguay /ˈpærəɡwaɪ; US ˈpærəɡweɪ/ **53**
parakeet /ˈpærəkiːt/ **93**/20
parallel /ˈpærəlel/ **47**/30
paramedic /ˌpærəˈmedɪk/ **38**/17
parcel /ˈpɑːsl/ **32**/1
parent /ˈpeərənt/ **1**/20
park /pɑːk/ **60**/2
parking lot /ˈpɑːkɪŋ lɒt/ **13**/15
parking notice /ˈpɑːkɪŋ nəʊtɪs/ **59**/2
parking sign /ˈpɑːrkɪŋ saɪn/ **59**/2
parrot /ˈpærət/ **93**/19
part /pɑːrt/ **5**/16
parting /ˈpɑːtɪŋ/ **5**/16
party /ˈpɑːti/ **71**/11
passenger /ˈpæsɪndʒə(r)/ **66**/20, **68**/2
passenger car /ˈpæsɪndʒər kɑːr/ **66**/4

passing lane /ˈpæsɪŋ leɪn/ **62**/17
passport /ˈpɑːspɔːt; US ˈpæspɔːrt/ **67**/6
passport control /ˌpɑːspɔːt kənˈtrəʊl; US ˌpæspɔːrt/ **67**/5
past /pɑːst; US pæst/ **37**/6-9, 14, 18
pâté /ˈpæteɪ; US pɑːˈteɪ/ **28**/4
path /pɑːθ; US pæθ/ **22**/23, **83**/5
patient /ˈpeɪʃnt/ **8**/3
patio /ˈpætiəʊ/ **22**/11
pattern /ˈpætn/ **9**
patterned /ˈpætnd/ **9**/21
pavement /ˈpeɪvmənt/ **59**/6
paw /pɔː/ **89**/24
pawpaw /ˈpɔːpɔː/ **24**/14
pay (verb) /peɪ/ **35**
pay in (verb) /ˌpeɪ ˈɪn/ **34**/17
paying-in slip /ˈpeɪɪŋ ɪn slɪp/ **34**/18
PC /ˌpiː ˈsiː/ **44**/25
pea /piː/ **28**/24
peach /piːtʃ/ **24**/11
peacock /ˈpiːkɒk/ **93**/24
peak /piːk/ **73**/2
peanut /ˈpiːnʌt/ **24**/5
pear /peə(r)/ **24**/16
pearl /pɜːl/ **91**/22
pedal /ˈpedl/ **65**/9
pedestrian /pəˈdestriən/ **60**/8
pedestrian crossing /pəˌdestriən ˈkrɒsɪŋ/ **59**/24
pelvis /ˈpelvɪs/ **4**/15
Pembrokeshire /ˈpembrʊkʃə(r)/ **56**
pen /pen/ **49**/22
pence /pens/ **36**/15-18
pence piece /ˌpens ˈpiːs/ **36**/2-7
pencil /ˈpensl/ **49**/20
pencil-sharpener /ˈpenslʃɑːpnə(r)/ **49**/25
penguin /ˈpeŋɡwɪn/ **93**/23
penknife /ˈpennaɪf/ **21**/4
Pennsylvania /ˌpensɪlˈveɪnjə/ **55**
penny /ˈpeni/ **35**/2, **36**/2
pepper /ˈpepə(r)/ **15**/16
per cent /pəˈsent/ **48**/17
percussion /pəˈkʌʃn/ **75**
perfume /ˈpɜːfjuːm; US also pərˈfjuːm/ **67**/11
perpendicular /ˌpɜːpənˈdɪkʊlə(r)/ **47**/29
Persian Gulf /ˌpɜːʃn ˈɡʌlf/ **54**
personal computer /ˌpɜːsənl kəmˈpjuːtə(r)/ **44**/25
personal stereo /pɜːsənl ˈsteriəʊ/ **30**/11
Perth and Kinross /ˌpɜːθ ənd kɪnˈrɒs/ **56**
Peru /pəˈruː/ **53**
pestle /ˈpesl; US ˈpestl/ **45**/7
pet /pet/ **89**
petal /ˈpetl/ **25**/4
Petri dish (US petri dish) /ˈpetri dɪʃ; US ˈpiːtri dɪʃ/ **46**/9
petrol pump /ˈpetrəl pʌmp/ **64**/11
pharmacist /ˈfɑːməsɪst/ **39**/6
pheasant /ˈfeznt/ **93**/7
Philadelphia /ˌfɪləˈdelfiə/ **55**
Philippines /ˈfɪlɪpiːnz/ **54**
Phoenix /ˈfiːnɪks/ **55**
phonecard /ˈfəʊnkɑːd/ **38**/24
photo album /ˈfəʊtəʊ ælbəm/ **29**/12
photographer /fəˈtɒɡrəfə(r)/ **40**/4
physical /ˈfɪzɪkl/ **5**
piano /piˈænəʊ/ **76**/3
piccolo /ˈpɪkələʊ/ **75**/10
pick up (verb) /pɪk ˈʌp/ **41**/6

pick-up truck /ˈpɪkʌp trʌk/ **63**/7
picnic /ˈpɪknɪk/ **71**/17
picture /ˈpɪktʃə(r)/ **49**/17, **58**/10
pie /paɪ/ **27**/11
piece /piːs/ **27**/10, 12, **49**/24, **86**/17-19
pier /pɪə(r)/ **60**/16
pigeon /ˈpɪdʒɪn/ **93**/14
pile /paɪl/ **26**/8
pill /pɪl/ **7**/7
pillar /ˈpɪlə(r)/ **14**/4
pillar-box /ˈpɪləbɒks/ **59**/3
pillow /ˈpɪləʊ/ **18**/12
pillowcase /ˈpɪləʊkeɪs/ **18**/7
pilot /ˈpaɪlət/ **68**/11
pin /pɪn/ **12**/22, **74**/16
pincer /ˈpɪnsə(r)/ **91**/19
pine cone /ˈpaɪn kəʊn/ **25**/22
pine tree /ˈpaɪn triː/ **25**/1
pineapple /ˈpaɪnæpl/ **24**/8
ping-pong /ˈpɪŋpɒŋ/ **78**/26
pink /pɪŋk/ **9**/2
pins /pɪnz/ **79**/10
pint /paɪnt/ **27**/24
pipette /pɪˈpet/ **46**/12
pitch /pɪtʃ/ **81**/16
pitcher /ˈpɪtʃər/ **15**/17
Pittsburgh /ˈpɪtsbɜːrɡ/ **55**
plaice /pleɪs/ **91**/10
plaid /plæd/ **9**/20
plain /pleɪn/ **9**/16
plait /plæt/ **5**/17
plane /pleɪn/ **21**/8, **68**/12
planet /ˈplænɪt/ **50**
plant /plɑːnt; US plænt/ **16**/19, **58**/11
plaster cast /ˌplɑːstə ˈkɑːst/ **7**/13
plate /pleɪt/ **15**/9, **58**/13, 15, 17
plateau /ˈplætəʊ; US plætəʊ/ **73**/18
platform /ˈplætfɔːm/ **66**/6
platform number /ˈplætfɔːm nʌmbə(r)/ **66**/18
play (verb) /pleɪ/ **42**/21
player /ˈpleɪə(r)/ **78**/17
playing-card /ˈpleɪɪŋkɑːd/ **74**/30
pliers /ˈplaɪəz/ **21**/6
plough (US plow) /plaʊ/ **73**/29
plug /plʌɡ/ **17**/7, **19**/12
plum /plʌm/ **24**/20
plumber /ˈplʌmə(r)/ **40**/10
plunger /ˈplʌndʒə(r)/ **45**/15
plus /plʌs/ **48**/11
Pluto /ˈpluːtəʊ/ **50**/15
Plymouth /ˈplɪməθ/ **56**
pm (US P.M.) /ˌpiːˈem/ **37**/16, 17, 18
pneumatic drill /njuːˌmætɪk ˈdrɪl; US nuːˌmætɪk ˈdrɪl/ **61**/16
pocket /ˈpɒkɪt/ **11**/18, **79**/7
pocketknife /ˈpɒkɪtnaɪf/ **21**/4
point /pɔɪnt/ **48**/11
Poland /ˈpəʊlənd/ **54**
polar bear /ˈpəʊlə beə(r)/ **90**/6
polaroid camera /ˌpəʊlərɔɪd ˈkæmərə/ **29**/23
pole /pəʊl/ **77**/8
police /pəˈliːs/ **38**
police car /pəˈliːs kɑː(r)/ **38**/2
police officer /pəˈliːs ɒfɪsə(r); US ɔːfɪsər/ **38**/3, **59**/5
police station /pəˈliːs steɪʃn/ **38**/1
polka-dot /ˈpɒlkədɒt; US ˈpəʊkədɒt/ **9**/18

# Index page 105

pond /pɒnd/ 73/23
pony /ˈpəʊnɪ/ 89/15
pony tail /ˈpəʊnɪ teɪl/ 5/13
pony-trekking /ˈpəʊnɪtrekɪŋ/ 72/16
Poole /puːl/ 56
pop group /ˈpɒp gruːp/ 76/7
porch /pɔːtʃ/ 14/16
port /pɔːt/ 69/70
porter /ˈpɔːtə(r)/ 71/2
portion /ˈpɔːʃn/ 27/10
Portland /ˈpɔːtlənd/ 55
Portsmouth /ˈpɔːtsməθ/ 56
Portugal /ˈpɔːtʃʊgl/ 54
post /pəʊst/ 31/10, 41/6
post office /ˈpəʊst ɒfɪs; US ɔː-/ 31/1
postal clerk /ˈpəʊstl klɑːrk/ 31/4
postal code /ˈpəʊstl kəʊd/ 32/13
postal order /ˈpəʊstl ɔːdə(r)/ 32/22
postal services /ˈpəʊstl ˌsɜːvɪsɪz/ 31/32
postbag /ˈpəʊstbæg/ 31/13
postbox /ˈpəʊstbɒks/ 31/11
postcard /ˈpəʊstkɑːd/ 32/8
postcode /ˈpəʊstkəʊd/ 32/13
poster /ˈpəʊstə(r)/ 18/15
postman /ˈpəʊstmən/ 31/8
postmark /ˈpəʊstmɑːk/ 32/12
pot /pɒt/ 20/26, 27/5, 19
pot holder /ˈpɒt həʊldər/ 20/21
potato /pəˈteɪtəʊ/ 23/9
potato chips /pəˈteɪtəʊ tʃɪps/ 26/16, 19
pottery /ˈpɒtərɪ/ 74/3
pouch /paʊtʃ/ 90/9
pound /paʊnd/ 36/18, 19
pound coin /ˌpaʊnd ˈkɔɪn/ 36/8-9
pound note /ˌpaʊnd ˈnəʊt/ 36/11-14
pour (verb) /pɔː(r)/ 83/11
power saw /ˈpaʊə sɔː/ 21/9
Powys /ˈpəʊɪs/ 56
pram /præm/ 60/3
praying mantis /ˌpreɪɪŋ ˈmæntɪs/ 92/19
preposition /ˌprepəˈzɪʃn/ 57/58
prescription /prɪˈskrɪpʃn/ 7/5
present /ˈpreznt/ 85/9, 10, 11
Princeton /ˈprɪnstən/ 55
print (verb) /prɪnt/ 43/11
print /prɪnt/ 9/21, 29/13, 14
printer /ˈprɪntə(r)/ 44/19
printout /ˈprɪntaʊt/ 44/18
prism /ˈprɪzm/ 45/12
promenade /ˌprɒməˈnɑːd; US ˈneɪd/ 72/5
propeller /prəˈpelə(r); US prəʊ-/ 68/15
protractor /prəˈtræktə(r); US prəʊ-/ 49/7
Providence /ˈprɒvɪdəns/ 55
Puerto Rico /ˌpwɜːtəʊ ˈriːkəʊ/ 53
pull (verb) /pʊl/ 86/22
pump /pʌmp/ 65/3
punch (verb) /pʌntʃ/ 79/22
punnet /ˈpʌnɪt/ 24/2
pupil /ˈpjuːpl/ 4/30, 49/2
puppy /ˈpʌpɪ/ 89/23
purple /ˈpɜːpl/ 9/10
purse /pɜːs/ 10/10, 11/22
push (verb) /pʊʃ/ 86/21
pushchair /ˈpʊʃtʃeə(r)/ 60/4
put down (verb) /ˌpʊt ˈdaʊn/ 86/16
pyjamas (US pajamas) /pəˈdʒɑːməz;
  US pəˈdʒæməz/ 11/14
pyramid /ˈpɪrəmɪd/ 47/23

Qatar /ˈkʌtɑː(r)/ 54
quarter /ˈkwɔːtə(r)/ 35/5, 37/8, 11, 48/19
queen /kwiːn/ 74/32
queue /kjuː/ 66/12
quiet /ˈkwaɪət/ 88/4

rabbit /ˈræbɪt/ 89/26
race (verb) /reɪs/ 80/24
race car /ˈreɪs kɑːr/ 80/7
race car driver /reɪs kɑːr draɪvər/ 12/1, 80/8
racecourse /ˈreɪskɔːs/ 80/28
racehorse /ˈreɪshɔːs/ 80/25
racetrack /ˈreɪstræk/ 80/6, 28
racing car /ˈreɪsɪŋ kɑː(r)/ 80/7
racing driver /ˈreɪsɪŋ draɪvə(r)/ 12/1, 80/8
rack /ræk/ 45/6
racket (also racquet) /ˈrækɪt/ 78/23
radiator /ˈreɪdɪeɪtə(r)/ 15/4
radiator grille /ˈreɪdɪeɪtə grɪl/ 64/18
radio /ˈreɪdɪəʊ/ 30/15
radio cassette recorder /reɪdɪəʊ kəˈset
  rɪˌkɔːdə(r)/ 30/8
radish /ˈrædɪʃ/ 23/6
radius /ˈreɪdɪəs/ 47/3
railings /ˈreɪlɪŋz/ 60/9
railroad /ˈreɪlrəʊd/ 66
railway /ˈreɪlweɪ/ 66
rain (verb) /reɪn/ 51/2
rainbow /ˈreɪnbəʊ/ 51/12
raincoat /ˈreɪnkəʊt/ 10/22
rainy /ˈreɪnɪ/ 51/2
rake /reɪk/ 22/7
ranch house /ˈræntʃ haʊs/ 14/19
raspberry /ˈrɑːzbrɪ; US ˈræzberɪ/ 28/10
razor /ˈreɪzə(r)/ 17/23
razor-blade /ˈreɪzəbleɪd/ 17/24
read (verb) /riːd/ 42/14, 85/12
Reading /ˈredɪŋ/ 56
rear-light /ˈrɪəˈlaɪt/ 64/8
receipt /rɪˈsiːt/ 29/2, 35/14
receiver /rɪˈsiːvə(r)/ 38/23
reception /rɪˈsepʃn/ 71/1
receptionist /rɪˈsepʃnɪst/ 71/4
record /ˈrekɔːd/ 30/5
recorder /rɪˈkɔːdə(r)/ 75/11
rectangle /ˈrektæŋgl/ 47/11
red /red/ 5/12, 9/1
Red Sea /ˌred ˈsiː/ 54/25
Redcar and Cleveland /ˈredkɑːr ənd
  ˈkliːvlənd/ 56
reel /riːl/ 26/1, 29/11, 74/11
referee /ˌrefəˈriː/ 79/25
reflector /rɪˈflektə(r)/ 65/14
refrigerator /rɪˈfrɪdʒəreɪtər/ 20/14
registered post /ˌredʒɪstəd ˈpəʊst/ 32/20
reins /reɪnz/ 80/14
remote control /rɪˌməʊt kənˈtrəʊl/ 16/9
Renfrewshire /ˈrenfruʃə(r)/ 56
Reno /ˈriːnəʊ/ 55
reptile /ˈreptaɪl/ 91
Republic of Ireland /rɪˌpʌblɪk əv ˈaɪələnd/
  56
reservoir /ˈrezəvwɑː(r)/ 73/13
restaurant /ˈrestrɒnt; US ˈrestərənt/ 28
return address /rɪˈtɜːn æˌdres/ 32/19
Réunion /riːˈjuːnjən/ 54
rhinoceros /raɪˈnɒsərəs/ 90/21
Rhode Island /ˌrəʊd ˈaɪlənd/ 55
Rhondda Cynon Taff /ˌrɒndə ˌkʌnən ˈtæf/ 56

rib /rɪb/ 4/13
ribbon /ˈrɪbən/ 58/2, 74/14
Richmond /ˈrɪtʃmənd/ 55
ride (verb) /raɪd/ 80/10
rider /ˈraɪdə(r)/ 80/11
riding /ˈraɪdɪŋ/ 80/9
right angle /ˈraɪt æŋgl/ 47/15
right lane /ˈraɪt leɪn/ 62/15
ring /rɪŋ/ 12/24, 79/19
ring binder /ˈrɪŋ baɪndə(r)/ 44/16
ring stand /ˈrɪŋ stænd/ 45/20
rink /rɪŋk/ 77/5
Rio Grande /ˌriːəʊ ˈgrænd/ 55
river /ˈrɪvə(r)/ 60/17
roach /rəʊtʃ/ 92/16
road /rəʊd/ 61/62, 62/24
road sign /ˈrəʊd saɪn/ 59/1, 61/62
road work /ˈrəʊd wɜːrk/ 61/13
roadworks /ˈrəʊdwɜːks/ 61/13
roast /ˈrəʊst/ 27/7
roast beef /ˌrəʊst ˈbiːf/ 28/16
roast chicken /ˌrəʊst ˈtʃɪkɪn/ 27/9
robe /rəʊb/ 11/13
Rochester /ˈrɒtʃɪstər/ 55
rock /rɒk/ 70/13, 73/9
rocket /ˈrɒkɪt/ 50/10
Rocky Mountains /ˌrɒkɪ ˈmaʊntnz/ 55
roll /rəʊl/ 26/1, 6, 15, 27/4, 29/11
rolling-pin /ˈrəʊlɪŋpɪn/ 20/12
Romania /ruːˈmeɪnɪə/ 54
roof /ruːf/ 13/2, 14/14, 23
room key /ˈruːm ˌkiː, ˈrʊm/ 71/5
rooster /ˈruːstər/ 93/4
root /ruːt/ 25/3
rope /rəʊp/ 79/20, 82/12
Roscommon /rɒsˈkɒmən/ 56
rose /rəʊz/ 25/17
rotary /ˈrəʊtərɪ/ 60/26
rotor /ˈrəʊtə(r)/ 68/11
rough /rʌf/ 88/15
round /raʊnd/ 58/2
round bottom flask /ˌraʊnd ˌbɒtəm ˈflɑːsk;
  US ˈflæsk/ 45/22
roundabout /ˈraʊndəbaʊt/ 60/26
row /rəʊ/ 26/7
rowboat /ˈrəʊbəʊt/ 69/7
rowing-boat /ˈrəʊɪŋbəʊt/ 69/7
rubber /ˈrʌbə(r)/ 49/26
rubber raft /ˈrʌbər ræft/ 70/14
rubber tubing /ˌrʌbə ˈtjuːbɪŋ; US ˌrʌbər
  ˈtuːbɪŋ/ 45/4
rucksack /ˈrʌksæk/ 66/16, 71/25
rug /rʌg/ 16/6
rugby /ˈrʌgbɪ/ 78/14
ruler /ˈruːlə(r)/ 49/21
run (verb) /rʌn/ 80/21
runner bean /ˈrʌnə biːn/ 28/23
runway /ˈrʌnweɪ/ 68/7
Russia /ˈrʌʃə/ 54
Russian Federation /ˌrʌʃn fedəˈreɪʃn/ 54
Rwanda /rʊˈændə/ 54

Sacramento /ˌsækrəˈmentəʊ/ 55
sad /sæd/ 88/2
saddle /ˈsædl/ 65/2, 80/12
safari /səˈfɑːrɪ/ 72/17
sail /seɪl/ 69/3
sailboard /ˈseɪlbɔːd/ 77/20
sailboat /ˈseɪlbəʊt/ 69/12

sailing /ˈseɪlɪŋ/ 72/10
sailing-ship /ˈseɪlɪŋ ʃɪp/ 69/1
sailor /ˈseɪlə(r)/ 39/11
Saint George's Channel /snt ˌdʒɔːˈdʒɪz ˈtʃænl/ 56
salad /ˈsæləd/ 28/22
salesperson /ˈseɪlzpɜːrsn/ 29/6
salmon /ˈsæmən/ 91/9
saloon /səˈluːn/ 63/12
salt /sɔːlt/ 15/15
Salt Lake City /ˌsɔːlt ˌleɪk ˈsɪtɪ/ 55
San Antonio /ˌsæn ænˈtəʊnɪəʊ/ 55
San Diego /ˌsæn dɪˈegəʊ/ 55
San Francisco /ˌsæn frænˈsɪskəʊ/ 55
San Jose /ˌsæn həʊˈzeɪ/ 55
sand /sænd/ 73/16
sandal /ˈsændl/ 12/8
sand-dune /ˈsænddjuːn; US duːn/ 73/17
sandpaper /ˈsændpeɪpə(r)/ 21/3
sandwich /ˈsænwɪdʒ; US -wɪtʃ/ 27/3
Santa Fe /ˌsæntəˈfeɪ/ 55
sash window /ˈsæʃ ˌwɪndəʊ/ 13/8
satellite /ˈsætəlaɪt/ 50/9
Saturday /ˈsætədɪ/ 33
Saturn /ˈsætɜːn/ 50/18
saucepan /ˈsɔːspən; US ˈsɔːspæn/ 20/26
saucer /ˈsɔːsə(r)/ 16/13
Saudi Arabia /ˌsaʊdɪ əˈreɪbɪə/ 54
Savannah /səˈvænə/ 55
saw /sɔː/ 21/9, 12, 20
saxophone /ˈsæksəfəʊn/ 75/16
scale /skeɪl/ 17/14, 31/2, 46/23, 53–56
scales /skeɪlz/ 17/14, 31/2, 46/23, 91/7
scar /skɑː(r)/ 6/21
scarf /skɑːf/ 10/14, 12/6
scenery /ˈsiːnərɪ/ 76/14
school bag /ˈskuːl bæg/ 49/8
school uniform /ˈskuːl ˈjuːnɪfɔːm/ 10/1
science laboratory /ˈsaɪəns ləˌbɒrətrɪ; US ˈlæbrətɔːrɪ/ 45/46
scissors /ˈsɪzəz/ 49/12
scooter /ˈskuːtə(r)/ 65/21
score (verb) /skɔː(r)/ 81/26
scorpion /ˈskɔːpɪən/ 92/23
Scotch tape /ˈskɒtʃ teɪp/ 26/1
Scotland /ˈskɒtlənd/ 56
Scottish Borders /ˌskɒtɪʃ ˈbɔːdəz/ 56
scourer /ˈskaʊərə(r)/ 20/6
scouring pad /ˈskaʊərɪŋ pæd/ 20/6
scratch /skrætʃ/ 6/17
screen /skriːn/ 44/26, 76/23
screw /skruː/ 21/22
screwdriver /ˈskruːdraɪvə(r)/ 21/21
scrub brush /ˈskrʌb brʌʃ/ 19/18
scrubbing-brush /ˈskrʌbɪŋbrʌʃ/ 19/18
scuba-diving /ˈskuːbədaɪvɪŋ/ 77/21
sea /siː/ 53, 73/8
Sea of Japan /ˌsiː əv dʒəˈpæn/ 54/36
Sea of Okhotsk /ˌsiː əv əʊˈkɒtsk/ 54/37
sea wall /siːˈwɔːl/ 72/4
seafront /ˈsiːfrʌnt/ 72/5
(sea)gull /ˈsiːgʌl/ 93/30
seal /siːl/ 90/27
seaside /ˈsiːsaɪd/ 72/1
season /ˈsiːzn/ 52
seat /siːt/ 57/3, 65/2, 23, 67/13
Seattle /sɪˈætl/ 55
second /ˈsekənd/ 33
second floor /ˌsekənd ˈflɔːr/ 13/13

second-class post /ˌsekəndklɑːs ˈpəʊst/ 32/15
second-hand /ˈsekəndhænd/ 37/5
secretary /ˈsekrətrɪ; US ˈsekrəterɪ/ 44/20
sector /ˈsektə(r)/ 47/6
security /sɪˈkjʊərətɪ/ 67/7
sedan /sɪˈdæn/ 63/12
Sellotape /ˈseləteɪp/ 26/1
semi-detached house /ˌsemɪdɪˌtætʃt ˈhaʊs/ 14/6
send (verb) /send/ 43/10
sender /ˈsendə(r)/ 32/18
Senegal /ˌsenɪˈgɔːl/ 54
September /sepˈtembə(r)/ 52
serve (verb) /sɜːv/ 81/2
server /ˈsɜːvə(r)/ 81/3
service area /ˈsɜːvɪs eərɪə/ 61/11
service line /ˈsɜːvɪs laɪn/ 81/5
service station /ˈsɜːvɪs steɪʃn/ 61/11
set /set/ 26/5
set square /ˈset skweə(r)/ 49/6
seven /ˈsevn/ 33/7
seventeen /ˌsevnˈtiːn/ 33/17
seventh /ˈsevnθ/ 33
seventy /ˈsevntɪ/ 33/70
sew (verb) /səʊ/ 83/4
sewing /ˈsəʊɪŋ/ 74/9
sewing-machine /ˈsəʊɪŋməˌʃiːn/ 74/10
shade /ʃeɪd/ 17/19
shake (verb) /ʃeɪk/ 85/1
shaker /ˈʃeɪkə(r)/ 74/27
shallow /ˈʃæləʊ/ 87/20
shampoo /ʃæmˈpuː/ 17/26
shape /ʃeɪp/ 47
shark /ʃɑːk/ 91/1
shaving cream /ˈʃeɪvɪŋ kriːm/ 17/25
shaving-foam /ˈʃeɪvɪŋfəʊm/ 17/25
shears /ʃɪəz/ 22/8
sheep /ʃiːp/ 89/9
sheet /ʃiːt/ 18/6, 31/18
sheet music /ˈʃiːt mjuːzɪk/ 76/6
Sheffield /ˈʃefiːld/ 56
shelf /ʃelf/ 20/23
shell /ʃel/ 91/26
Shetland Islands /ˈʃetlənd ˌaɪləndz/ 56
ship /ʃɪp/ 70/5
shirt /ʃɜːt/ 10/19
shock absorber /ˈʃɒk əbˌzɔːbə(r)/ 65/29
shoe /ʃuː/ 10/23
shoelace /ˈʃuːleɪs/ 11/23
shoot (verb) /ʃuːt/ 78/10
shop /ʃɒp/ 59/12
shop assistant /ˈʃɒp əˌsɪstənt/ 29/6
short /ʃɔːt/ 5/8, 9, 10, 11, 19
shorts /ʃɔːts/ 12/12
shoulder /ˈʃəʊldə(r)/ 3/6, 62/14, 23
shower /ˈʃaʊə(r)/ 17/20, 41/7
shrimp /ʃrɪmp/ 91/17
Shropshire /ˈʃrɒpʃə(r)/ 56
shutter /ˈʃʌtə(r)/ 14/5
shuttlecock /ˈʃʌtlkɒk/ 78/25
side /saɪd/ 47/10, 48/9
side mirror /ˈsaɪd mɪrə(r)/ 64/2
side street /ˈsaɪd striːt/ 60/5
sideboard /ˈsaɪdbɔːd/ 15/18
sideline /ˈsaɪdlaɪn/ 81/6
sidewalk /ˈsaɪdwɔːk/ 59/6
Sierra Leone /sɪˌerə lɪˈəʊn/ 54
Sierra Nevada /sɪˌerə nəˈvɑːdə/ 55

sieve /sɪv/ 20/2
sightseeing /ˈsaɪtsiːɪŋ/ 71/9
sign (verb) /saɪn/ 43/6
sign /saɪn/ 57/9, 10
signal tower /ˈsɪgnəl taʊər/ 66/1
signal-box /ˈsɪgnəl bɒks/ 66/1
signature /ˈsɪgnətʃə(r)/ 43/7
signpost /ˈsaɪnpəʊst/ 60/23
sing (verb) /sɪŋ/ 85/6
Singapore /ˌsɪŋəˈpɔː(r)/ 54
singer /ˈsɪŋə(r)/ 76/9
single lens reflex camera /ˌsɪŋgl lenz ˈriːfleks ˌkæmərə/ 29/16
single room /ˈsɪŋgl ˈruːm, ˈrʊm/ 71/6
singles match /ˈsɪŋglz mætʃ/ 81/1
sink /sɪŋk/ 17/6, 19/2
Sioux Falls /ˌsuː ˈfɔːlz/ 55
sister /ˈsɪstə(r)/ 1/11
sister-in-law /ˈsɪstər ɪn lɔː/ 1/13
sit (verb) /sɪt/ 84/21
six /sɪks/ 33/6
sixteen /ˌsɪksˈtiːn/ 33/16
sixth /sɪksθ/ 33
sixty /ˈsɪkstɪ/ 33/60
skate (verb) /skeɪt/ 77/2
skater /ˈskeɪtə(r)/ 77/3
skeleton /ˈskelɪtn/ 4/10
ski (verb) /skiː/ 77/7
ski /skɪː/ 77/9
skiing /ˈskiːɪŋ/ 77/6
skip (verb) /skɪp/ 82/27
skipping-rope /ˈskɪpɪŋrəʊp/ 82/26
skirt /skɜːt/ 10/11
skull /skʌl/ 4/11
sky /skaɪ/ 60/13
skyline /ˈskaɪlaɪn/ 60/14
skyscraper /ˈskaɪskreɪpər/ 60/12
slate /sleɪt/ 13/2, 20
sleep (verb) /sliːp/ 84/24
sleeping-bag /ˈsliːpɪŋ bæg/ 71/21
sleeve /sliːv/ 11/16
slice /slaɪs/ 27/8
slide /slaɪd/ 29/9, 46/20
slide projector /ˈslaɪd prəˌdʒektə(r)/ 29/8
Sligo /ˈslaɪgəʊ/ 56
sling /slɪŋ/ 7/11
slip-road /ˈslɪprəʊd/ 62/2
slipper /ˈslɪpə(r)/ 11/12
slot /slɒt/ 38/25
Slovakia /sləʊˈvækɪə/ 54
Slovenia /sləʊˈviːnɪə/ 54
slow /sləʊ/ 87/24
slow lane /ˈsləʊ leɪn/ 62/5, 15
SLR camera /ˌes el ˈɑː ˌkæmərə/ 29/16
slug /slʌg/ 92/21
small /smɔːl/ 87/4
smile (verb) /smaɪl/ 84/17
smoke /sməʊk/ 38/7
smoked salmon /ˌsməʊkt ˈsæmən/ 28/3
smokestack /ˈsməʊkstæk/ 70/10
smooth /smuːð/ 88/16
snail /sneɪl/ 92/22
snake /sneɪk/ 91/27
sneaker /ˈsniːkər/ 12/4
snooker /ˈsnuːkə(r)/ 79/4
snorkel /ˈsnɔːkl/ 77/24
snorkelling (US snorkeling) /ˈsnɔːklɪŋ/ 77/23
snout /snaʊt/ 91/5
snow (verb) /snəʊ/ 51/3

snow /snəʊ/ 51/4
snowy /'snəʊɪ/ 51/3
soap /səʊp/ 17/8
soccer /'sɒkər/ 81'
sock /sɒk/ 11/4
socket /'sɒkɪt/ 19/21
Socotra /sə'kəʊtrə/ 54
soda /'səʊdə/ 27/26
sofa /'səʊfə/ 16/17
soft /sɒft/ 88/18
soil /sɔɪl/ 61/19, 83/7
solar system /'səʊlə sɪstəm/ 50
soldier /'səʊldʒə(r)/ 39/12
solid /'sɒlɪd/ 9/16, 88/22
solid figure /sɒlɪd 'fɪɡə(r); US 'fɪɡjər/ 47/20
Solomon Islands /'sɒləmən ˌaɪləndz/ 54
Somalia /sə'mɑːlɪə/ 54
Somerset /'sʌməset/ 56
son /sʌn/ 1/16
sore /sɔː(r)/ 6/8
sound system /saʊnd ˌsɪstəm/ 30/13
soup /suːp/ 28/5
south /saʊθ/ 56
South Africa /ˌsaʊθ 'æfrɪkə/ 54
South China Sea /ˌsaʊθ ˌtʃaɪnə 'siː/ 54/33
South Georgia /ˌsaʊθ 'dʒɔːrdʒə/ 53
South Korea /ˌsaʊθ kə'rɪə/ 54
Southampton /saʊθ'æmptən/ 56
space /speɪs/ 50
space shuttle /speɪs ʃʌtl/ 50/11
spacesuit /'speɪssuːt/ 50/7
spade /speɪd/ 22/19, 74/34
Spain /speɪn/ 54
spanner /'spænə(r)/ 21/27
sparrow /'spærəʊ/ 93/15
spatula /'spætʃʊlə/ 46/10
speak (verb) /spiːk/ 85/5
speaker /'spiːkə(r)/ 30/10
Special Delivery /speʃl dɪ'lɪvərɪ/ 32/24
spectator /spek'teɪtə(r); US 'spek-/ 80/18
speed limit /'spiːd lɪmɪt/ 61/6
speedometer /spiː'dɒmɪtə(r)/ 64/24
spider /'spaɪdə(r)/ 92/11
spine /spaɪn/ 4/14
spiral /'spaɪərəl/ 47/28
spirit-level /'spɪrɪtlevl/ 21/7
spoke /spəʊk/ 65/7
sponge /spʌndʒ/ 17/12
spool /spuːl/ 74/11
spoon /spuːn/ 15/11
sport /spɔːt/ 77–81
sports car /'spɔːts kɑː(r)/ 63/11
sports centre /'spɔːts sentə(r)/ 42/19
sprain (verb) /spreɪn/ 6/14
spring /sprɪŋ/ 52/9
spring balance /ˌsprɪŋ 'bæləns/ 46/24
square /skweə(r)/ 47/9
squash /skwɒʃ/ 42/21, 78/22
squid /skwɪd/ 91/14
squirrel /'skwɪrəl/ 89/6
Sri Lanka /ˌʃriː 'læŋkə/ 54
St Lawrence /seɪnt 'lɒrəns/ 55
St Louis /seɪnt 'luːɪs/ 55
St Paul /seɪnt 'pɔːl/ 55
stack /stæk/ 24/22
Staffordshire /'stæfədʃə(r)/ 56
stage /steɪdʒ/ 46/19, 76/15
stair /steə(r)/ 18/22

staircase /'steəkeɪs/ 18/25
stall /stɔːl/ 23/1
stalls /stɔːlz/ 76/20
stamp /stæmp/ 31/19
stamp album /'stæmp ælbəm/ 74/5
stamp collecting /'stæmp kəˌlektɪŋ/ 74/4
stamp machine /'stæmp məˌʃiːn/ 31/17
stand (verb) /stænd/ 84/22
stand /stænd/ 23/1, 81/24
staple (verb) /'steɪpl/ 43/4
stapler /'steɪplə(r)/ 44/12
star /stɑː(r)/ 50/26
starfish /'stɑːfɪʃ/ 91/20
start (verb) /stɑːt/ 42/15
starter /'stɑːtə(r)/ 28
starting-block /'stɑːtɪŋ blɒk/ 80/22
starting-gate /'stɑːtɪŋ geɪt/ 80/27
state line /ˌsteɪt 'laɪn/ 55
station /'steɪʃn/ 66
station wagon /'steɪʃn ˌwægən/ 63/14
stationery /'steɪʃənrɪ; US–nerɪ/ 26
steak /steɪk/ 28/18
steering-wheel /'stɪərɪŋ wiːl; US also hwiːl/ 64/22
stem /stem/ 25/19
step /step/ 18/22, 57/11, 13
stereo /'sterɪəʊ/ 30/13
stereo system /'sterɪəʊ ˌsɪstəm/ 30/13
stern /stɜːn/ 69/17
stethoscope /'steθəskəʊp/ 7/20
steward /'stjʊəd/ 67/13
stick /stɪk/ 78/18
(sticking-)plaster /'stɪkɪŋplɑːstə(r)/ 7/3
sting /stɪŋ/ 92/24
stir (verb) /stɜː(r)/ 83/12
Stirling /'stɜːlɪŋ/ 56
stirrup /'stɪrəp/ 80/13
stockings /'stɒkɪŋz/ 11/6
Stockton-on-Tees /ˌstɒktən ɒn 'tiːz/ 56
Stoke-on-Trent /ˌstəʊk ɒn 'trent/ 56
stomach /'stʌmək/ 3/25, 4/8
stomach-ache /'stʌməkeɪk/ 6/5
stone /stəʊn/ 13/17
stone wall /ˌstəʊn 'wɔːl/ 14/18
stool /stuːl/ 45/19
stop /stɒp/ 61/2
stop clock /stɒp klɒk/ 46/16
stopper /'stɒpə(r)/ 17/7, 46/4
store /stɔːr/ 29, 59/12
stormy /'stɔːmɪ/ 51/9
Strabane /strə'bæn/ 56
straight /streɪt/ 5/8, 9, 47/26, 87/1
strainer /'streɪnər/ 20/2
Strait of Dover /ˌstreɪt əv 'dəʊvə(r)/ 56
strap /stræp/ 29/22
Stratford-upon-Avon /ˌstrætfəd əpɒn 'eɪvən/ 56
strawberry /'strɔːbrɪ; US 'strɔːberɪ/ 24/2
stream /striːm/ 73/7
street /striːt/ 59/10
street corner /ˌstriːt 'kɔːnə(r)/ 59/11
street sign /striːt saɪn/ 60/10
stretch (verb) /stretʃ/ 82/19
stretcher /'stretʃə(r)/ 38/16
string /strɪŋ/ 26/2
string bean /ˌstrɪŋ 'biːn/ 28/23
strings /strɪŋz/ 75
striped /straɪpt/ 9/17
stroller /'strəʊlər/ 60/4

strong /strɒŋ/ 87/22
student /'stjuːdnt/ 49/2
stuffed olives /ˌstʌft 'ɒlɪvz/ 27/23
stumps /stʌmps/ 81/19
suburbs /sʌ'bɜːbz/ 60
subway /sʌbweɪ/ 66
Sudan /suː'dɑːn; US suː'dæn/ 54
Suffolk /'sʌfək/ 56
suit /suːt/ 10/18
suitcase /'suːtkeɪs/ 66/14, 86/13–16
summer /'sʌmə(r)/ 52/10
Sun /sʌn/ 50/14
sun-glasses /'sʌnglɑːsɪz; US -glæsɪz/ 12/18
sunbather /'sʌnbeɪðə(r)/ 72/8
sunbed /'sʌnbed/ 72/7
sunburn /'sʌnbɜːn/ 6/16
Sunday /'sʌndɪ/ 33
sunny /'sʌnɪ/ 51/1
sunshade /'sʌnʃeɪd/ 72/9
surf (verb) /sɜːf/ 77/15
surfboard /'sɜːfbɔːd/ 77/17
surfer /'sɜːfə(r)/ 77/16
surfing /'sɜːfɪŋ/ 77/13
surgeon /'sɜːdʒən/ 7/18
Suriname /ˌsʊərɪ'næm/ 53
Surrey /'sʌrɪ/ 56
Sussex /'sʌsɪks/ 56
swallow /'swɒləʊ/ 93/21
swan /swɒn/ 93/31
Swansea /'swɒnzɪ/ 56
Swaziland /'swɑːzɪlænd/ 54
sweater /'swetə(r)/ 10/6
sweatshirt /'swetʃɜːt/ 12/14
Sweden /'swiːdn/ 54
sweep (verb) /swiːp/ 83/5
sweet corn /'swiːt kɔːn/ 28/20
sweets /swiːts/ 26/10, 14, 15, 18
swim (verb) /swɪm/ 77/26
swimmer /'swɪmə(r)/ 77/27
swimming /'swɪmɪŋ/ 77/25
swimming-pool /'swɪmɪŋ puːl/ 77/28
swimming-trunks /'swɪmɪŋ trʌŋks/ 11/1
swimsuit /'swɪmsuːt/ 11/2
swing (verb) /swɪŋ/ 82/11
swing /swɪŋ/ 22/2
Switzerland /'swɪtsələnd/ 54
synthesizer /'sɪnθəsaɪzə(r)/ 76/13
Syracuse /'sɪrəkjuːs/ 55
Syria /'sɪrɪə/ 54
syringe /sɪrɪndʒ/ 45/16

T-shirt /'tiːʃɜːt/ 10/5
table /'teɪbl/ 57/8, 58/4, 5, 6, 79/6
table tennis /'teɪbl tenɪs/ 78/26
table-cloth /'teɪblklɒθ/ 15/8
tablet /'tæblɪt/ 7/7
tackle (verb) /'tækl/ 78/15
tail /teɪl/ 68/18, 89/17, 91/2
taillight /'teɪllaɪt/ 64/8
Taiwan /taɪ'wɑːn/ 54
Tajikistan /tæ'dʒiːkɪstɑːn/ 54
take (verb) /teɪk/ 41/7, 85/10
take-off /'teɪkɒf/ 68/6
talc /tælk/ 17/28
talcum powder /'tælkəm paʊdə(r)/ 17/28
talk (verb) /tɔːk/ 85/5
tall /tɔːl/ 5/18
tambourine /ˌtæmbə'riːn/ 75/18

Tampa /'tæmpə/ 55
tank top /'tæŋk tɒp/ 12/10
tanker /'tæŋkə(r)/ 63/3
Tanzania /ˌtænzə'nɪə/ 54
tape /teɪp/ 32/2
tape deck /'teɪp dek/ 30/18
tape-measure /'teɪpˌmeʒə(r)/ 74/13
tartan /'tɑːtn/ 9/20
Tasman Sea /ˌtæzmən 'siː/ 54/31
taxi /'tæksɪ/ 60/6
tea /tiː/ 83/12
tea towel /'tiː taʊəl/ 20/7
teacher /'tiːtʃə(r)/ 49/16
teapot /'tiːpɒt/ 16/11, 58/16, 17, 83/11
tear (verb) /teə(r)/ 86/18
teaspoon /'tiːspuːn/ 16/15
teenage /'tiːneɪdʒ/ 5/3
teenager /'tiːneɪdʒə(r)/ 5/3
(tele)phone booth /'telɪfəʊn buːθ/ 38/22
(tele)phone box /'telɪfəʊn bɒks/ 38/22
(tele)phone number /'telɪfəʊn nʌmbə(r)/ 38/21
telescope /'telɪskəʊp/ 29/5
television /'telɪvɪʒn/ 16/23, 42/23, 58/18
teller /'telə(r)/ 34/9
temperature /'temprətʃə(r); US 'tempərtʃʊər/ 6/10, 52
ten /ten/ 33/10
Tennessee /ˌtenə'siː/ 55
tennis /'tenɪs/ 81
tennis-court /'tenɪsˌkɔːt/ 81/10
tent /tent/ 71/19
tentacle /'tentəkl/ 91/13
tenth /tenθ/ 33
terminal /'tɜːmɪnl/ 67
terraced house /'terəst ˌhaʊs/ 13/1
test-tube /'test tjuːb; US 'test tuːb/ 45/2
Texas /'teksəs/ 55
textbook /'tekstbʊk/ 49/3
Thailand /'taɪlænd/ 54
thatch /θætʃ/ 13/21
thatched roof /ˌθætʃt 'ruːf/ 14/14
theatre (US theater) /'θɪətə(r)/ 76
thermometer /θə'mɒmɪtə(r)/ 45/21
thick /θɪk/ 87/13
thimble /'θɪmbl/ 74/17
thin /θɪn/ 5/20, 87/14
third /θɜːd/ 33, 48/20
thirsty /'θɜːstɪ/ 6/1
thirteen /ˌθɜː'tiːn/ 33/13
thirteenth /ˌθɜː'tiːnθ/ 33
thirtieth /'θɜːtɪəθ/ 33
thirty /'θɜːtɪ/ 33/30
thirty-first /ˌθɜːtɪ'fɜːst/ 33
thousand /'θaʊzənd/ 33/1000
thread /θred/ 74/11, 20
three /θriː/ 33/3
three quarters /ˌθiː 'kwɔːtəz/ 48/22
throat /θrəʊt/ 3/27, 6/8
throttle /'θrɒtl/ 65/26
through /θruː/ 57/3
throw (verb) /θrəʊ/ 57/4, 5, 78/13, 82/9
thumb /θʌm/ 3/21
thunderstorm /'θʌndəstɔːm/ 51/10
Thursday /'θɜːzdɪ/ 33
ticket counter /'tɪkɪt kaʊntər/ 66/10
ticket office /'tɪkɪt ɒfɪs/ 66/14
ticket taker /'tɪkɪt teɪkər/ 66/19
ticket-collector /ˌtɪkɪtkə'lektə(r)/ 66/19

tidy /'taɪdɪ/ 88/7
tie /taɪ/ 10/20
tie up (verb) /ˌtaɪ 'ʌp/ 83/6
tiger /'taɪgə(r)/ 90/17
tight /taɪt/ 88/23
tights /taɪts/ 11/7
tile /taɪl/ 13/19, 17/2
(tiled) floor /ˌtaɪld 'flɔː(r)/ 49/9
tiled roof /ˌtaɪld 'ruːf/ 14/23
time /taɪm/ 37
timer /'taɪmər/ 46/16
times /taɪmz/ 48/13
timetable /'taɪmteɪbl/ 66/15
tin /tɪn/ 27/6
tin-opener /'tɪn əʊpənə(r)/ 20/10
Tipp-Ex /'tɪpeks/ 44/9
Tipperary /ˌtɪpə'reərɪ/ 56
tired /'taɪəd/ 6/3
tissues /'tɪʃuːz/ 18/9
to /tuː, tʊ/ 37/10, 11, 12, 57/6
toast /təʊst/ 28/4
toaster /'təʊstə(r)/ 20/17
toe /təʊ/ 3/14
Togo /'təʊgəʊ/ 54
toilet /'tɔɪlɪt/ 17/17
toilet paper /'tɔɪlɪt ˌpeɪpə(r)/ 17/18
Toledo /tə'liːdəʊ/ 55
tomato /tə'mɑːtəʊ; US te'meɪtəʊ/ 23/19
tongs /tɒŋz/ 45/13
tongue /tʌŋ/ 4/22
tool /tuːl/ 21
tool-box /'tuːlbɒks/ 21/1
tooth /tuːθ/ 8/8
toothache /'tuːθeɪk/ 6/4
toothbrush /'tuːθbrʌʃ/ 17/4
toothpaste /'tuːθpeɪst/ 17/3
top box /'tɒp bɒks/ 65/24
top case /'tɒp keɪs/ 65/24
top floor /ˌtɒp 'flɔː(r)/ 13/11
Topeka /tə'piːkə/ 55
torch /tɔːtʃ/ 19/17
Torfaen /ˌtɔː'vaɪn/ 56
tortoise /'tɔːtəs/ 91/25
total /'təʊtl/ 35/15
tour guide /'tʊə gaɪd; Brit also 'tɔː/ 71/10
tourist /'tʊərɪst/ Brit also 'tɔːrɪst/ 71/12
toward /tɔːd/ 57/10
towards /tə'wɔːdz/ 57/10
towel rack /'taʊəl ræk/ 17/9
towel-rail /'taʊəlreɪl/ 17/9
tower block /'taʊə blɒk/ 60/12
town /taʊn/ 55/56
town house /'taʊn haʊs/ 13/1
trachea /trə'kɪə; US 'treɪkɪə/ 4/2
track /træk/ 80/17, 66/7
track and field /træk ənd fiːld/ 80/15
track number /'træk ˌnʌmbər/ 66/18
track suit /'træk suːt/ 12/3
tractor /'træktə(r)/ 73/28
traffic /'træfɪk/ 59/13
traffic circle /'træfɪk sɜːrkl/ 60/26
traffic-lights /'træfɪklaɪts/ 60/19
trailer /'treɪlə(r)/ 63/9, 68/3, 71/27
trailer camp /'treɪlər kæmp/ 71/26
train /treɪn/ 42/13, 66/8
trainer /'treɪnə(r)/ 12/4
tramline /'træmlaɪn/ 81/6
trampoline /'træmpəliːn/ 82/6
trampolining /ˌtræmpə'liːnɪŋ/ 82/4

transporter /træn'spɔːtə(r)/ 63/1
trash can /'træʃ kæn/ 57/4, 59/14
travel agent /'trævl eɪdʒənt/ 40/3
traveller's cheque (US traveler's check) /'trævləz tʃek/ 34/10, 11
tray /treɪ/ 16/12
tree /triː/ 22/4, 25/1, 57/3
triangle /'traɪæŋgl/ 47/13, 49/6
tricycle /'traɪsɪkl/ 65/17
Trinidad and Tobago /ˌtrɪnɪdæd ənd tə'beɪgəʊ/ 53
triple-pack /'trɪplpæk/ 26/13
tripod /'traɪpɒd/ 29/4, 45/26
trolley /'trɒlɪ/ 28/6, 46/15, 67/18, 86/21
trombone /trɒm'bəʊn/ 75/5
tropic of Cancer /ˌtrɒpɪk əv 'kænsə(r)/ 53/54
tropic of Capricorn /ˌtrɒpɪk əv 'kæprɪkɔːn/ 53/54
trousers /'traʊzəz/ 10/4
trout /traʊt/ 28/17, 91/8
trowel /'traʊəl/ 22/12
truck /trʌk/ 63/4
truck driver /'trʌk draɪvər/ 40/2
trumpet /'trʌmpɪt/ 75/7
trunk /trʌŋk/ 25/2, 64/9, 90/26
tub /tʌb/ 27/20
tuba /'tjuːbə; US 'tuːbə/ 75/9
tube /tjuːb; US tuːb/ 17/3
Tucson /'tuːsɒn/ 55
Tuesday /'tjuːzdɪ/ 33
tulip /'tjuːlɪp; US 'tuːlɪp/ 25/25
Tulsa /'tʌlsə/ 55
tuna /'tjuːnə; US 'tuːnə/ 27/6, 18
Tunisia /tjuː'nɪzɪə; US tuː'nɪʒə/ 54
tunnel /'tʌnl/ 66/9
Turkey /'tɜːkɪ/ 54
turkey /'tɜːkɪ/ 93/6
Turkmenistan /tɜːk'miːnɪstɑːn/ 54
turn right /ˌtɜːn 'raɪt/ 61/12
turn signal /'tɜːrn ˌsɪgnəl/ 64/3
turnip /'tɜːnɪp/ 23/18
turntable /'tɜːnteɪbl/ 30/14
turquoise /'tɜːkwɔɪz/ 9/8
turtle /'tɜːtl/ 91/24
tusk /tʌsk/ 90/25
TV /ˌtiː 'viː/ 16/23, 42/23
TV aerial /ˌtiː 'viː eəriəl/ 14/20
twelfth /twelfθ/ 33
twelve /twelv/ 33/12
twentieth /'twentɪəθ/ 33
twenty /'twentɪ/ 33/20
twenty-first /ˌtwentɪ'fɜːst/ 33
twenty-one /ˌtwentɪ'wʌn/ 33/21
twenty-second /ˌtwentɪ'sekənd/ 33
twenty-third /ˌtwentɪ'θɜːd/ 33
twin beds /ˌtwɪn 'bedz/ 71/8
Twin Falls /ˌtwɪn 'fɔːlz/ 55
twin room /ˌtwɪn 'ruːm, 'rʊm/ 71/8
twin-pack /ˌtwɪnˌpæk/ 26/12
two /tuː/ 33/2
two-family house /'tuːˌfæməlɪ ˌhaʊs/ 14/6
two-way traffic /ˌtuːweɪ 'træfɪk/ 61/4
Tyne and Wear /ˌtaɪn ənd 'wɪə(r)/ 56
type (verb) /taɪp/ 43/3
typewriter /'taɪpraɪtə(r)/ 44/27
tyre (US tire) /'taɪə(r)/ 65/27

U-tube /'juːtjuːb; US 'juːtuːb/ 45/18
Uganda /juː'gændə/ 54

UK /ˌjuːˈkeɪ/ **56**
Ukraine /juːˈkreɪn/ **54**
umbrella /ʌmˈbrelə/ **10**/16
umpire /ˈʌmpaɪə(r)/ **81**/11, 20
uncle /ˈʌŋkl/ **1**/4
under /ˈʌndə(r)/ **58**/5
underground /ˈʌndəɡraʊnd/ **66**
underneath /ˌʌndəˈniːθ/ **58**/5
underpants /ˈʌndəpænts/ **11**/10
underpass /ˈʌndəpɑːs; US -pæs/ **62**/21
underwear /ˈʌndəweə(r)/ **11**/3
unhappy /ʌnˈhæpɪ/ **88**/2
unitary authority /ˌjuːnətri ɔːˈθɒrəti/ **56**
United Arab Emirates /juːˌnaɪtɪd ˌærəb ˈemɪrəts/ **54**
United Kingdom /juːˌnaɪtɪd ˈkɪŋdəm/ **56**
United States of America /juːˌnaɪtɪd ˌsteɪts əv əˈmerɪkə/ **55**
untidy /ʌnˈtaɪdɪ/ **88**/8
up /ʌp/ **57**/11
upstairs /ˌʌpˈsteəz/ **18**/24
Uranus /ˈjʊrənəs/ **50**/17
Uruguay /ˈjʊərəɡwaɪ; US ˈjʊərəɡweɪ/ **53**
US /ˌjuːˈes/ **55**
USA /ˌjuːˈesˈeɪ/ **55**
usher /ˈʌʃə(r)/ **76**/25, 26
usherette /ˌʌʃəˈret/ **76**/26
Utah /ˈjuːtɔː/ **55**
utility room /juːˈtɪlətɪ ˌruːm, ˌrʊm/ **19**
Uzbekistan /ʊzˈbekɪstɑːn/ **54**

vacation /veɪˈkeɪʃn/ **71**/72
vacuum cleaner /ˈvækjuːm ˌkliːnə(r)/ **19**/7
Vale of Glamorgan /ˌveɪl əv ɡləˈmɔːɡən/ **56**
valley /ˈvælɪ/ **73**/3
valve /vælv/ **65**/11
van /væn/ **31**/7, **63**/5
Vanuatu /ˌvænʊˈɑːtuː/ **54**
vase /vɑːz; US veɪs, veɪz/ **15**/20
vault (verb) /vɔːlt/ **82**/16
vaulting-horse /ˈvɔːltɪŋhɔːs/ **82**/18
VCR /ˌviːsiːˈɑː(r)/ **16**/24
vegetable /ˈvedʒtəbl/ **23**, **28**
vehicle /ˈviːəkl; US ˈviːhɪkl/ **63**
venetian blind /vəˌniːʃn ˈblaɪnd/ **44**/17
Venezuela /ˌvenɪzˈweɪlə/ **53**
Venus /ˈviːnəs/ **50**/22
verb /vɜːb/ **43**, **83–86**
Vermont /vərˈmɒnt/ **55**
vest /vest/ **12**/10
vet /vet/ **40**/6
vice (US vise) /vaɪs/ **21**/11
video cassette recorder /ˌvɪdɪəʊ kəˈset rɪˌkɔːdə(r)/ **16**/24
(video)tape /ˈvɪdɪəʊteɪp/ **30**/4
Vietnam /ˌvjetˈnæm; US ˌvjetˈnɑːm/ **54**
viewfinder /ˈvjuːˌfaɪndə(r) /**30**/3
village /ˈvɪlɪdʒ/ **71**/15
viola /vɪˈəʊlə/ **75**/1
violin /ˌvaɪəˈlɪn/ **75**/4
Virginia /vərˌdʒɪnjə/ **55**
vocalist /ˈvəʊkəlɪst/ **76**/9
volleyball /ˈvɒlɪbɔːl/ **78**/20

waist /weɪst/ **3**/24
waiter /ˈweɪtə(r)/ **28**/14
waiting area /ˈweɪtɪŋ eərɪə/ **67**/12
wake up (verb) /ˌweɪk ˈʌp/ **41**/1

Wales /weɪlz/ **56**
walk (verb) /wɔːk/ **57**/2, 9–11, 13, **82**/1
walk /wɔːk/ **83**/5
Walkman /ˈwɔːkmən/ **30**/11
wall /wɔːl/ **15**/2, **22**/25, **57**/12
wall bars /ˈwɔːl bɑːz/ **82**/14
wall unit /ˈwɔːl juːnɪt/ **16**/21
wallet /ˈwɒlɪt/ **11**/21, 22
wardrobe /ˈwɔːdrəʊb/ **18**/17
warehouse /ˈweəhaʊs/ **70**/3
warm /wɔːm/ **52**/4
Warwickshire /ˈwɒrɪkʃə(r)/ **56**
wash (verb) /wɒʃ/ **84**/13
wash-basin /ˈwɒʃbeɪsn/ **17**/6
washcloth /ˈwɒːʃklɒθ/ **17**/13
washer /ˈwɒʃər; US ˈwɔːʃər/ **21**/26
washing-machine /ˈwɒʃɪŋməˌʃiːn; US ˈwɔːʃɪŋməˌʃiːn/ **19**/3
washing-up liquid /ˌwɒʃɪŋˈʌp lɪkwɪd/ **20**/5
Washington /ˈwɒʃɪŋtən/ **55**
Washington DC /ˌwɒʃɪŋtən ˌdiːˈsiː/ **55**
wasp /wɒsp/ **92**/3
waste-paper basket /ˌweɪstˈpeɪpə bɑːskɪt; US ˌweɪstˈpeɪpər bæskɪt/ **16**/16
watch (verb) /wɒtʃ/ **42**/23
watch /wɒtʃ/ **12**/15
water /ˈwɔːtə(r)/ **38**/6, **83**/10, 11
water-ski (verb) /ˈwɔːtəskiː/ **77**/11
water-skier /ˈwɔːtəskiːə(r)/ **77**/12
water-skiing /ˈwɔːtəskiːɪŋ/ **77**/10
watercress /ˈwɔːtəkres/ **23**/13
waterfall /ˈwɔːtəfɔːl/ **73**/6
Waterford /ˈwɔːtəfəd/ **56**
watering-can /ˈwɔːtərɪŋkæn/ **22**/6
wave (verb) /weɪv/ **85**/4
wave /weɪv/ **77**/14
wavy /ˈweɪvɪ/ **5**/11
weak /wiːk/ **87**/21
weather /ˈweðə(r)/ **51**
webbed foot /ˌwebd ˈfʊt/ **93**/29
Wednesday /ˈwenzdɪ/ **33**
week /wiːk/ **37**
weight /weɪt/ **46**/13, **48**/23
welder /ˈweldə(r)/ **40**/9
west /west/ **56**
West Indies /ˌwest ˈɪndɪz/ **53**
West Midlands /ˌwest ˈmɪdləndz/ **56**
Western Isles /ˌwestən ˈaɪls/ **56**
wet /wet/ **88**/10
Wexford /ˈweksfəd/ **56**
whale /weɪl; US also hweɪl/ **90**/30
wheel /wiːl; US also hwiːl/ **65**/20
wheelbarrow /ˈwiːlbærəʊ; US also ˈhwiːlbærəʊ/ **22**/17
wheelchair /ˈwiːltʃeə(r); US also ˈhwiːltʃeər/ **7**/15
whisker /ˈwɪskər; US also ˈhwɪskər/ **89**/19
whistle /ˈwɪsl; US also ˈhwɪsl/ **82**/24
white /waɪt; US also hwaɪt/ **9**/14
Wichita /ˈwɪtʃɪtɑː/ **55**
wicket /ˈwɪkɪt/ **81**/19
wicket-keeper /ˈwɪkɪtkiːpə(r)/ **81**/13
Wicklow /ˈwɪkləʊ/ **56**
wide /waɪd/ **87**/15
width /wɪdθ, wɪtθ/ **48**/3
wife /waɪf/ **1**/12
Wiltshire /ˈwɪltʃə(r)/ **56**
wind up (verb) /ˌwaɪnd ˈʌp/ **83**/8

window /ˈwɪndəʊ/ **14**/8, **31**/5, **57**/1, **58**/1, **66**/11, **83**/3
window-box /ˈwɪndəʊbɒks/ **13**/3
window-ledge /ˈwɪndəʊledʒ/ **14**/9
window-sill /ˈwɪndəʊsɪl/ **14**/9
windpipe /ˈwɪndpaɪp/ **4**/2
windscreen /ˈwɪndskriːn/ **64**/19
windscreen wiper /ˈwɪndskriːn ˌwaɪpə(r)/ **64**/10
windshield /ˈwɪndʃiːld/ **64**/19
windshield wiper /ˈwɪndʃiːld ˌwaɪpər/ **64**/10
windsurfer /ˈwɪndsɜːfə(r)/ **77**/19
windsurfing /ˈwɪndsɜːfɪŋ/ **77**/18
windy /ˈwɪndɪ/ **51**/5
wing /wɪŋ/ **68**/16, **93**/17
wing mirror /ˈwɪŋ mɪrə(r)/ **64**/2
wings /wɪŋz/ **76**/18
winter /ˈwɪntə(r)/ **52**/12
wire /ˈwaɪə(r)/ **46**/5
wire mesh screen /ˌwaɪər ˈmeʃ skriːn/ **45**/25
Wisconsin /wɪsˈkɒnsɪn/ **55**
witch /wɪtʃ/ **12**/16
withdraw (verb) /wɪðˈdrɔː/ **34**/15
withdrawal slip /wɪðˈdrɔːəl slɪp/ **34**/19
wolf /wʊlf/ **90**/3
woman /ˈwʊmən/ **5**/4
wood /wʊd/ **13**/22, **73**/19
wooden gate /ˈwʊdn ˈɡeɪt/ **14**/17
woodwind /ˈwʊdwɪnd/ **75**
wool /wʊl/ **74**/22
work /wɜːk/ **42**/15, 18
work surface /ˈwɜːk ˌsɜːfɪs/ **20**/13
workbench /ˈwɜːkbentʃ/ **21**/5
worm /wɜːm/ **92**/20
wrapping paper /ˈræpɪŋ ˌpeɪpə(r)/ **26**/6
wrench /rentʃ/ **21**/19, 27
wrestle (verb) /ˈresl/ **79**/24
wrestling /ˈreslɪŋ/ **79**/23
Wrexham /ˈreksəm/ **56**
wrist /rɪst/ **3**/23
writing-paper /ˈraɪtɪŋˌpeɪpə(r)/ **26**/4
Wyoming /waɪˈəʊmɪŋ/ **55**

X-ray (also x-ray) /ˈeksreɪ/ **8**/10
X-ray scanner /ˈeksreɪ ˌskænə(r)/ **67**/9

yacht /jɒt/ **69**/12
year /jɪə(r), also jɜː(r)/ **37**
yellow /ˈjeləʊ/ **9**/5
Yellow Sea /ˌjeləʊ ˈsiː/ **54**/35
Yemen Republic /ˌjemən rɪˈpʌblɪk/ **54**
yield /jiːld/ **61**/1
yoghurt /ˈjɒɡət/ **27**/19, 27
yogurt /ˈjəʊɡərt/ **27**/19, 27
York /jɔːk/ **56**
Yorkshire /ˈjɔːkʃə(r)/ **56**
young /jʌŋ/ **5**/2
Yugoslavia /ˌjuːɡəʊˈslɑːvɪə/ **54**

Zambia /ˈzæmbɪə/ **54**
zebra /ˈzebrə, ˈziːbrə/ **90**/15
zero /ˈzɪərəʊ/ **52**/8
Zimbabwe /zɪmˈbɑːbwɪ/ **54**
zip /zɪp/ **74**/12
zip code /ˈzɪp kəʊd/ **32**/16
zipper /ˈzɪpər/ **74**/12
zoom lens /ˈzuːm lenz/ **29**/15
zucchini /zʊˈkiːnɪ/ **23**/12

# People and Health Pages 1-8

## 1 Who's who?

Read the sentences about this family and then write the names in the family tree.

 = is married to

Peter is married to Ann and they have a daughter called Laura.
Peter's parents are Jack and Rosy.
Ann's sister, Sarah, has a son called Leo.

Linda is Ann's sister-in-law.
Alan's mother-in-law is called Joan.
Jamie is Leo's cousin.
Bill has got two grandsons and one granddaughter.

Peter

## 2 The Human Body

There are sixteen parts of the body hidden in this square. Can you find them all?

*thumb*

_____    _____    _____

_____    _____    _____

_____    _____    _____

_____    _____    _____

_____    _____    _____

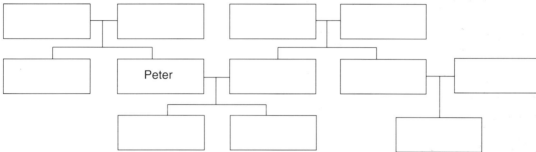

| e | i | b | h | e | a | d | e | n | o | x |
|---|---|---|---|---|---|---|---|---|---|---|
| o | y | u | e | a | m | o | o | a | t | s |
| t | o | e | o | u | b | i | f | i | s | t |
| a | e | z | o | m | e | f | i | l | o | o |
| n | c | a | u | e | c | a | n | g | e | m |
| k | e | h | i | e | a | h | g | i | i | a |
| l | t | e | i | o | u | e | e | i | o | c |
| e | e | a | o | n | a | i | r | s | e | h |
| u | l | u | o | e | t | x | u | e | t | e |
| a | i | b | a | c | k | a | e | e | i | e |
| e | p | a | i | k | n | e | e | t | e | k |

## 3 What's the matter?

Match what the patient says to the doctor's advice.

Patient

a   I have dreadful earache.
b   I've got a sore throat and a temperature.
c   I've fallen over and hurt my arm.
d   I've got a small scratch on my leg.
e   I've got terrible toothache.

a _3_   b ___   c ___   d ___   e ___

Doctor

1   Take two of these tablets and go straight to bed.
2   You probably need a filling.
3   Put two drops in each ear twice a day.
4   We'll need to put it in a sling.
5   Put some of this ointment on it and then cover it with a plaster.

# Exercises

## Clothes Pages 9-12

**1 Test your memory!**

Look carefully at page 10.

Fill in the missing words in the sentences below. Use words from the box.

a   The woman is wearing a _____

blouse and a _____ blue jacket.

b   The boy is wearing a _____

blazer and _____ trousers.

c   The man is wearing a red and white

_____ tie and he is carrying a

raincoat.

d   The girl is wearing a _____ coat

and a _____ scarf.

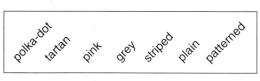

polka-dot   tartan   pink   grey   striped   plain   patterned

■ *Language note*

The man in the picture is **wearing** a suit and he is **carrying** a raincoat.

**2   What other things are people carrying in the picture? Write some sentences.**

_____

_____

_____

_____

_____

**3   Match each of these words with the right part of the body.**

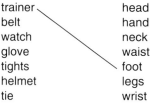

| trainer | head |
| belt | hand |
| watch | neck |
| glove | waist |
| tights | foot |
| helmet | legs |
| tie | wrist |

**4   Find the words from the mixed-up letters. They are all things that people wear or carry. When you have finished, read down the box to find the mystery word.**

1   FRIEHCEKHDAN
2   FRASC
3   LABRUMEL
4   ERUPS
5   RECIFEABS
6   RENGIRA
7   LACKENCE
8   NABAHGD
9   GIRN
10  LOSECAHE
11  LAWLET
12  GESSNALUSS

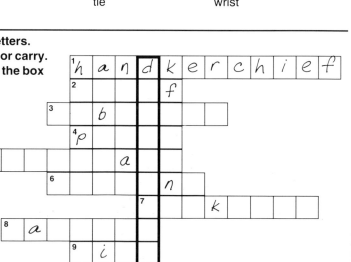

# At Home Pages 15-22 and 58

**1    Find the word in each group that is different from the others.**

**a**    mug   cup   freezer   saucer   teapot

**b**    scales   aftershave   soap   shampoo   toothpaste

**c**    wardrobe   sideboard   vase   wall unit   chest of drawers

**d**    duster   brush   scourer   oven   mop

**e**    rake   watering-can   shears   lawnmower   bush

**2    Write in the words.**

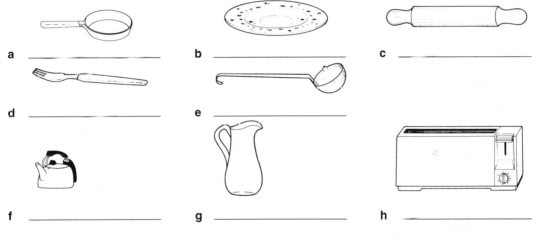

a  _____    b  _____    c  _____

d  _____    e  _____

f  _____    g  _____    h  _____

**3    Test your memory!**

Look at page 18 for two minutes, then read these sentences about the picture. Decide if they are true or false.

**a**    The box of tissues is in the bedside cabinet.
**b**    There's a poster over the bed.
**c**    There's a hair-drier on the dressing table.
**d**    The dressing table is in front of the chest of drawers.
**e**    The blanket is under the bedspread.
**f**    There's a coat-hanger betweeen the light and the alarm clock.

If the sentences are false, write them correctly.

_____

_____

_____

_____

# Exercises page 113

## Shopping and Food Pages 23-28

**1** **Match a word in A with the right word in B.**

A | B
--- | ---
a tube of | chocolate
a loaf of | cereal
a bar of | toothpaste
a bottle of | margarine
a jar of | jam
a packet of | bread
a tub of | biscuits
a box of | mineral water

**2** **Complete these dialogues using words from the box. Use each word only once.**

1 a  Can I help you?

  b  Yes, please. How much are the

    _____ ?

  a  They're 70p a bunch.

  b  And the strawberries?

  a  85p a _____ .

2 a  I'd like some _____

    for my wife's birthday.

  b  Certainly, sir. Any particular kind?

  a  Well, yes, she likes these blue ones.

  b  Oh, you mean _____ .

3 a  I'm looking for a _____

    of chocolates. Have you got any?

  b  They're up on the top

    _____ .

  a  They're a present for somebody so I'll

    need a roll of _____

    and a _____ of

    Sellotape too, please.

4 a  Are you ready to order? Here comes the

    _____ .

  b  No, I haven't decided yet. Are you going

    to have a _____ ?

  a  Yes, I think I'll have the melon.

| flowers   bananas   starter   shelf   punnet   waiter   wrapping paper   irises   box   reel |
| --- |

**3** **Where do each of the conversations in exercise 2 take place?**

1  _____     3  _____

2  _____     4  _____

# Dates and Times Pages 33 and 37

**1** **Look at the clocks, then find two ways of saying each time, using the expressions in the box.**

1  _c,_ _____  2  _____

3  _____  4  _____

5  _____  6  _____

| a | midnight |
| b | ten to five |
| c | eleven fifty-five |
| d | four fifty |
| e | a quarter to three in the afternoon |
| f | six thirty pm |
| g | seven minutes past four |
| h | two forty-five pm |
| i | half past six in the evening |
| j | twelve o'clock at night |
| k | five to twelve |
| l | four o seven |

**2** **Dates**

John always forgets important dates so he writes them down at the beginning of the year in a special page in his diary.

Look at the page, then answer the questions by writing the dates **in words**.

**Important dates 1998**

16/1  Mum's birthday

1/5  holiday (3 weeks)

3/8  Aunt Edna arrives from Australia

12/9  our wedding anniversary

22/11 – 30/11  exams!

**a**  When is John's mother's birthday?
_____

**b**  When does John's holiday begin?
_____

**c**  On what date does Aunt Edna arrive?
_____

**d**  When is John's wedding anniversary?
_____

**e**  On what date do his exams finish?
_____

# At Work Pages 39-40 and 43-44

## 1 What do we call someone who...

...reads the news aloud on the radio or TV?

_____

...arranges people's holidays for them?

_____

...works with wood?

_____

... makes bread and cakes?

_____

...treats sick animals?

_____

...repairs cars?

_____

## 2 Read these job advertisements and decide what job is being offered in each one.

**a** Ladies' and gentlemen's ***** needed for modern salon. Experience of cutting all types of hair necessary.

**b** ***** for long-distance deliveries. Must have licence.

**c** WANTED! Qualified ***** for small chemist's. Duties to include dispensing prescriptions plus general shop work.

**d** EXPERIENCE IN RADIO? Love all kinds of music? 'Joy FM' is looking for a *****.

a _____

b _____

c _____

d _____

## 3 Office wordsearch

There are thirteen words connected with the office in this square. Can you find them all?

| e | a | n | d | i | s | k | a | i | l | s |
|---|---|---|---|---|---|---|---|---|---|---|
| i | o | c | h | e | q | u | e | o | e | i |
| u | b | o | i | e | s | y | f | u | t | w |
| f | c | t | t | a | i | k | d | n | t | a |
| t | i | e | y | u | n | r | i | g | e | a |
| e | u | l | p | e | e | r | a | c | r | i |
| i | e | i | e | l | p | u | r | d | x | x |
| n | g | r | p | i | u | o | y | a | e | u |
| e | c | a | o | o | i | e | f | m | i | o |
| s | t | e | o | x | p | u | u | o | y | e |
| s | n | o | t | e | b | o | o | k | a | e |

*cheque*

_____

_____

_____

_____

_____

_____

_____

_____

_____

_____

_____

_____

# Describing Things Pages 47-49 and 87-88

**1** **Write the names of these shapes.**

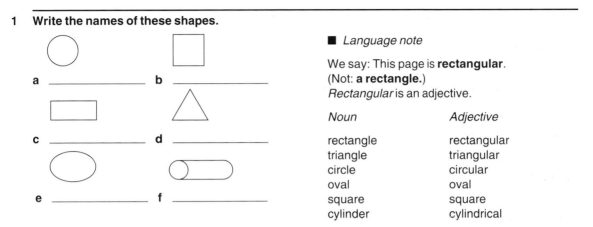

a _____  b _____

c _____  d _____

e _____  f _____

■ *Language note*

We say: This page is **rectangular**.
(Not: **a rectangle**.)
*Rectangular* is an adjective.

| Noun | Adjective |
|------|-----------|
| rectangle | rectangular |
| triangle | triangular |
| circle | circular |
| oval | oval |
| square | square |
| cylinder | cylindrical |

**2** **Match these questions and answers by writing the correct number next to the questions.**

*Question*

a   What shape is it?

b   How much does it weigh?

c   How big is it?

d   What's it made of?

e   What's it used for?

*Answer*

1   It's used for measuring things and for drawing straight lines.

2   This one is made of plastic but they are also made of wood.

3   It's rectangular.

4   About 10g.

5   It's about 15 cm long, 3 cm wide and 0.2 cm thick.

**What is it? It's on page 49 of this dictionary.** _____

**3** **Find the opposites of these adjectives and write them in the puzzle.**

1   crooked
2   thin
3   light
4   tight
5   empty
6   hollow
7   dry

**Now read down the box to find another adjective!**

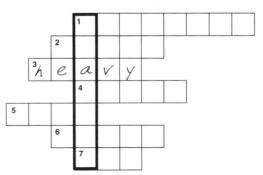

# Exercises

## The Weather Pages 51-52 and 56

1 **Look at the weather map of the British Isles below. Find a symbol for each of the words in the box and draw it.**

| | | |
|---|---|---|
| sun | cloud | rain |
| wind | fog | snow |

■ *Language note*

The adjective from { **cloud** is **cloudy**.
                    { **sun** is **sunny**.

Make adjectives from the other words in the box. (If you are not sure about the spelling, check on page 51.)

wind    _____

snow    _____

fog     _____

rain    _____

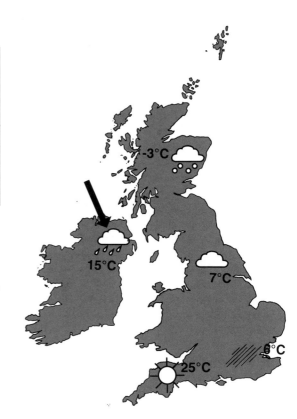

2 **Look at the weather map and write in the missing information below.**

*Tomorrow's Weather*

The South-East will start the day quite

(1) _____ and

(2) _____, but in the

South-West it's going to be rather

(3) _____ and

(4) _____. Further north it will

be (5) _____ all day with a

maximum (6) _____ of 7°C.

Over in Northern Ireland it will be

(7) _____ with some

(8) _____ during the morning and it

will be very (9) _____ on the coast.

Up in Scotland the temperature will fall to

(10) _____ 3°C and there may be

some (11) _____ .

# The City Pages 57 and 59-60

### 1 Letter-box or mailbox?

These are six things that you can find in a city street. Complete the table by writing the British or American words.

| British | American |
|---|---|
| letter-box | |
| | sidewalk |
| crossroads | |
| | traffic circle |
| | trash can |
| pedestrian crossing | |

### 2 Look at the pictures and complete the sentences using words from the box.

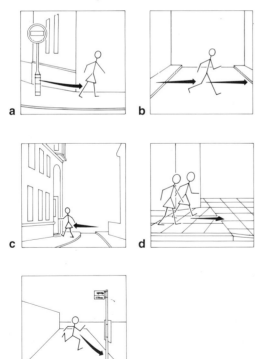

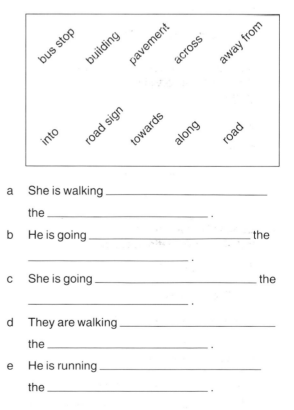

bus stop    building    pavement    across    away from

into    road sign    towards    along    road

a   She is walking _____

the _____ .

b   He is going _____ the

_____ .

c   She is going _____ the

_____ .

d   They are walking _____

the _____ .

e   He is running _____

the _____ .

# Exercises

## Travelling Pages 63-68

**1 Label these pictures.**

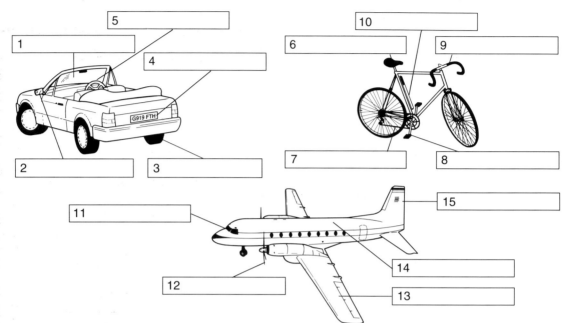

| | |
|---|---|
| 5 | 10 |
| 1 | 6 · 9 |
| 4 | |
| 2 · 3 | 7 · 8 |

| | |
|---|---|
| 11 | 15 |
| 12 | 14 |
| | 13 |

---

**2 Airport crossword**

*Across*

1 ____ pass
5

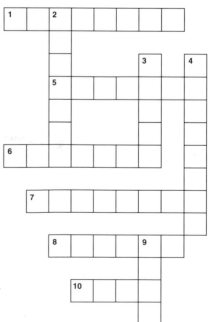

6 ____ desk
  (where you go to collect your *1 across*)
7

8 departure ____
10 You sit on this.

*Down*

2 ____ ticket
3 The part of the plane where the passengers are.
4 You can find an X-ray scanner here.
9 'Your flight is now boarding at ____ six.'

# On Holiday Pages 71-73

**Read the hotel information, look at the pictures, and fill in the missing words.**

## ✳ Sunnyview Hotel - information

Please leave your [1] _ _ _ _ _ _ _ at the hotel reception when you go out.

Thank you.

★★★★★★★★★★★★★★★★★★★★★★★★★★

### Activities

Dalton Lake is only half a mile from the hotel. There you can go [2] _ _ _ _ _ or [3] _ _ _ _ _ _ _ _.

Northend-by-the-sea is a pretty holiday resort. Go [4] _ _ _ _ _ along the cliffs or just sit on the [5] _ _ _ _ _ and enjoy the sun!

If you want to do something really exciting, why not try [6] _ _ _ _ _ _ _ _ or even [7] _ _ _ _ - _ _ _ _ _ _ _?

★★★★★★★★★★★★★★★★★★★★★★★★★★

### SIGHTSEEING

Monday: Visit to Longleat, a historic [8] _ _ _ _ _ _ _ _ _ _ _ _ _ in Wiltshire.

Wednesday: A tour of the local countryside. A [9] _ _ _ _ _ _ is provided.

Friday: Coach trip to a beautiful [10] _ _ _ _ _ _ _ _ _ _ _.

Bring your camera!

# Exercises page 121

# Music and Theatre Pages 75-76

**1** Write the names of these instruments. The words are in the box, but the letters of each word have been mixed up.

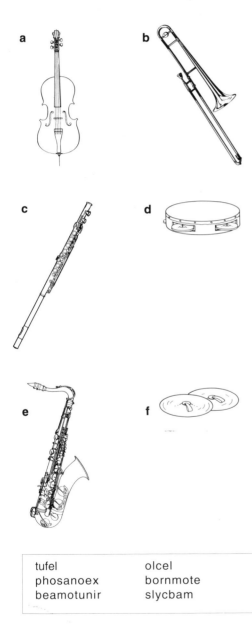

a

b

c

d

e

f

| | |
|---|---|
| tufel | olcel |
| phosanoex | bornmote |
| beamotunir | slycbam |

**2** What's the word?

a You walk along this to get to your seat in a cinema or a theatre.

— — — — —

b He or she helps you to find your seat.

— — — — —

c Somebody who plays a large percussion instrument.

— — — — — — —

d Where the orchestra sits.

— — —

e The American word for a 'balcony' in a cinema or a theatre.

— — — — — — — —

f Actors and actresses wait here before they go on stage.

— — — — —

g A word that means 'singer'.

— — — — — — —

h Things on the stage of a theatre that make it look like a real place.

— — — — — —

Now take the first letter of each of the words you found for **a**, **b** and **c**, the second letter of **d** and **e** and the third letter of **f**, **g** and **h**. You will then have the word for a group of people who are watching a film or a play!

_____

# Sports Pages 77-81

1  **Fill in the table using words from the box.
   Use each word only once.**

| Sport | Person | Place | Equipment |
|-------|--------|-------|-----------|
|  |  | *court* |  |
|  | *caddy* |  |  |
| *cricket* |  |  |  |
|  |  | *track* |  |
|  |  |  | *starting-gate* |

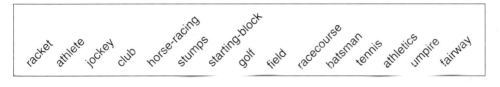

racket    athlete    jockey    club    horse-racing    stumps    starting-block    golf    field    racecourse    batsman    tennis    athletics    umpire    fairway

2  **Sports Quiz**

a   Name three sports in which players **tackle** each other.

_____

b   What is the other name for **ping-pong**?

_____

c   Name three objects that you need for playing baseball.

_____

d   In which sport do players use **sticks**?

_____

e   Name a sport that takes place under water.

_____

f   Name three sports that need a **net**.

_____

# Exercises page 123

## Verbs Pages 83-86

**1  What shall I do now?**

Bob never knows what to do. Give him
some advice by writing the correct numbers by
the letters.

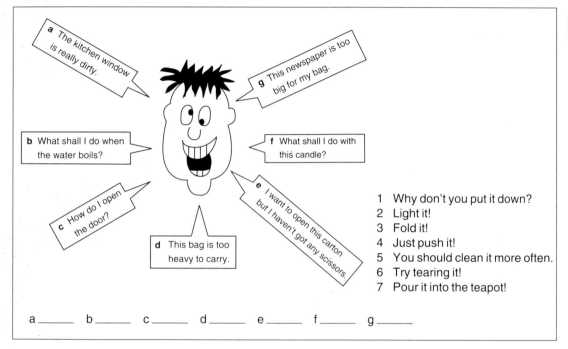

**a** The kitchen window is really dirty.

**g** This newspaper is too big for my bag.

**b** What shall I do when the water boils?

**f** What shall I do with this candle?

**c** How do I open the door?

**e** I want to open this carton but I haven't got any scissors.

**d** This bag is too heavy to carry.

1  Why don't you put it down?
2  Light it!
3  Fold it!
4  Just push it!
5  You should clean it more often.
6  Try tearing it!
7  Pour it into the teapot!

a _____  b _____  c _____  d _____  e _____  f _____  g _____

**2  Match these verbs to the right thing or person.**

You can...

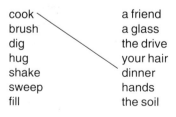

| | |
|---|---|
| cook | a friend |
| brush | a glass |
| dig | the drive |
| hug | your hair |
| shake | dinner |
| sweep | hands |
| fill | the soil |

# Animals

Pages 89-93

### Wordsnake
Complete the puzzle with the first letter of each word at the correct number. Every answer except the first begins with the last letter of the word before it.

1. An insect with hard wings.
2. A large grey animal with a trunk.
3. A wild animal with yellow fur and black stripes.
4. It's got a horn on its nose.
5. This small animal has got a big tail and lives in trees.
6. A reptile with a long body usually seen in hot, dry places.
7. A young one of these is called a puppy.
8. It has a very long neck.
9. It looks like a snake and lives in water.
10. A young sheep.
11. A large black animal with horns found mainly in Asia and Africa.
12. It has got eight 'arms'.
13. We get wool from these.
14. A large animal with black and white fur.
15. A very small insect.

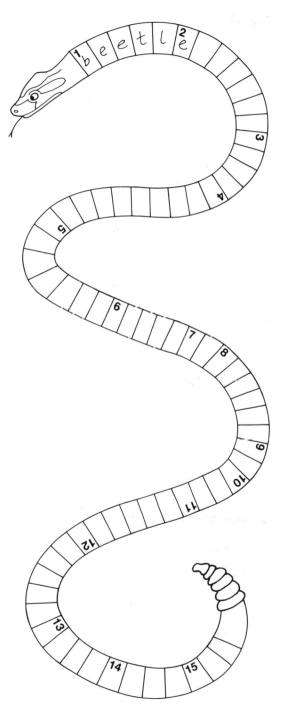

# Key to exercises

## People and Health page 110

1
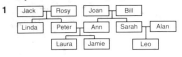

2  ankle, back, cheek, chest, chin, eye,
finger, fist, head, knee, lip, nail, neck,
stomach, toe

3  **b** 1  **c** 4  **d** 5  **e** 2

## Clothes page 111

1  **a** patterned, plain  **b** striped, grey
**c** polka-dot  **d** pink, tartan

2  The girl is carrying an umbrella.
The woman is carrying a handbag and
a briefcase.
The man is carrying a sweater.

3  belt - waist, watch - wrist, glove - hand,
tights - legs, helmet - head, tie - neck

4  2. scarf  3. umbrella  4. purse
5. briefcase  6. earring  7. necklace
8. handbag  9. ring  10. shoelace
11. wallet  12. sun-glasses
**dressing gown**

## At Home page 112

1  **a** freezer  **b** scales  **c** vase  **d** oven
**e** bush

2  **a** frying-pan  **b** plate  **c** rolling-pin
**d** fork  **e** ladle  **f** kettle  **g** jug
**h** toaster

3  **a** *false*. The box of tissues is on the
bedside cabinet.  **b** *true*.  **c** *false*.
There's a hair-drier on the chest of
drawers.  **d** *false*. The dressing table
is next to the chest of drawers.  **e** *true*.
**f** *false*. There's a poster between the
light and the alarm clock.

## Shopping and Food page 113

1  loaf of bread, bar of chocolate, bottle of
mineral water, jar of jam, packet of
biscuits, tub of margarine,  box of cereal

2  1. bananas, punnet  2. flowers, irises
3. box, shelf, wrapping paper, reel
4. waiter, starter

3  1. market  2. florist's  3. newsagent's
4. restaurant

## Dates and Times page 114

1  1. c, k  2. f, i  3. g, l  4. a, j  5. b, d
6. e, h

2  **a** On the sixteenth of April/ April the
sixteenth.  **b** On the first of May/ May
the first.  **c** On the third of August/
August the third.  **d** On the twelfth of
September/ September the twelfth.
**e** On the thirtieth of November/
November the thirtieth.

## At Work page 115

1  newsreader, travel agent, carpenter,
baker, vet, mechanic

2  **a** hairdresser  **b** lorry driver
**c** pharmacist  **d** disc jockey

3  desk, diary, disk, fax, file, letter,
notebook, pen, print, screen, stapler,
type

## Describing Things page 116

1  **a** circle  **b** square  **c** rectangle
**d** triangle  **e** oval  **f** cylinder

2  **a** 3  **b** 4  **c** 5  **d** 2  **e** 1  It's a **ruler**.

3  1. straight  2. thick  4. loose  5. full
6. solid  7. wet  **shallow**

## The Weather page 117

1
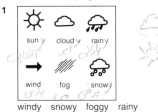

windy  snowy  foggy  rainy

2  1. cold  2. foggy  3. warm  4. sunny
5. cloudy  6. temperature  7. cool
8. rain  9. windy  10. minus
11. snow

## The City page 118

1  mailbox, pavement, intersection,
roundabout, litter-bin, crosswalk

2  **a** away from, road sign  **b** across, road
**c** into, building  **d** along, pavement
**e** towards, bus stop

## Travelling page 119

1  1. windscreen  2. wing mirror  3. tyre
4. number-plate  5. steering-wheel
6. saddle  7. chain  8. pedal
9. handlebar  10. pump  11. cockpit
12. propeller  13. wing  14. fuselage
15. tail

2  1. boarding  2. airline  3. cabin
4. security  5. luggage  6. check-in
7. passport  8. lounge  9. gate
10. seat

## On Holiday page 120

1. room key  2. sailing  3. fishing
4. hiking  5. beach  6. ballooning
7. hang-gliding  8. country house
9. picnic  10. waterfall

## Music and Theatre page 121

1  **a** cello  **b** trombone  **c** flute
**d** tambourine  **e** saxophone
**f** cymbals

2  **a** aisle  **b** usher  **c** drummer  **d** pit
**e** mezzanine  **f** wings  **g** vocalist
**h** scenery  **audience**

## Sports page 122

1

| Sport | Person | Place | Equipment |
|---|---|---|---|
| tennis | umpire | court | racket |
| golf | caddy | fairway | club |
| cricket | batsman | field | stumps |
| athletics | athlete | track | starting-block |
| horse-racing | jockey | racecourse | starting-gate |

2  **a** rugby, hockey, football
**b** table tennis
**c** batting helmet, baseball glove/mitt,
face mask/catcher's mask
**d** hockey  **e** scuba-diving
**f** basketball, volleyball, badminton, *or*
tennis

## Verbs page 123

1  **a** 5  **b** 7  **c** 4  **d** 1  **e** 6  **f** 2  **g** 3

2  brush your hair, dig the soil, hug a friend,
shake hands, sweep the drive, fill a glass

## Animals page 124

1. beetle  2. elephant  3. tiger
4. rhinoceros  5. squirrel  6. lizard
7. dog  8. giraffe  9. eel  10. lamb
11. buffalo  12. octopus  13. sheep
14. panda  15. ant